D1558885

"The world was peopled
with wonders."

The origin of Wildsam comes from above, a
line of prose in the novel *East of Eden*, written by
John Steinbeck. Six words hinting at a broad and
interwoven idea. One of curiosity, connection, joy. And
the belief that stories have the power to unearth the
mysteries of a place—for anyone. The book in
your hands is rooted in such things.

Our deepest thanks to all those who helped us bring the City of
Brotherly Love to life in these pages. Our research benefited
from the smart work of local journalists and historians who
contribute to excellent city publications including *Philadelphia*
magazine, *The Philadelphia Inquirer* and *Hidden City Daily*.
We're grateful for insight, tips and cheesesteak preferences
from Elena Gooray, Alex Lewis, Emma Copley Eisenberg,
Alexander Schneider, Christina Rosso-Schneider,
Caitlin Martin and Gia Vecchio.

WILDSAM FIELD GUIDES™

Copyright © 2020

Published in the United States
by Wildsam Field Guides, Austin, Texas.

ISBN 978-1-4671-9907-0

Illustrations by Derick Jones

To find more field guides, please visit
www.wildsam.com

CONTENTS

*Discover the people and places
that tell the story of Philadelphia*

ESSENTIALS 006

*Trusted intel and travel info about iconic places
and important topics*

BESTS...013

*Selected recommendations for the most authentic
Philadelphia experiences*

ALMANAC 023

*Archival excerpts, timelines, clippings and
other historical musings*

MAPS..051

*Illustrated renderings of subject matter vital
to the city's heart and soul*

INTERVIEWS..071

*Concise and meaningful one-way conversations
with locals of note*

STORIES..095

*Personal essays about the city from respected
Philly writers*

INDEX 121

NOTES 126

FOLDOUT MAP 145

WELCOME

WHEN FAIRGOERS STEPPED inside the Philadelphia "Workingman's House" model at the 1893 World's Columbian Exposition in Chicago, the story goes, they found it such a marvel that their footsteps wore out the floorboards. What struck them wasn't any architectural flourish, but rather the sense of efficiency and sheer possibility: The modest two-story dwelling could be purchased for $2,500. A tidy, realizable dream. In Philadelphia, row houses like these were already granting hardworking people the chance not just to make a living, but to build a life.

This is a city of neighborhoods: Its residents aren't just proud to be from Philly [though they don't take kindly to "Sixth Borough" of New York jokes]. They're proud to be from Manayunk, Kensington, Mount Airy, Point Breeze. And more than that, it's a city of neighborliness— thanks, in no small part, to the row house. Walk the streets of Old City or East Passyunk and you'll see versions of these buildings everywhere: block after block of narrow houses, no more than four stories, each one attached to the next. Row homes make up 70 percent of Philadelphia's housing. And they knit neighborliness into the city's very fabric.

Living on a block of row houses means lives constantly intersect. It means greeting the kids on the stoop next door as they slurp melting water ice on a blazing July day. It means shoveling an elderly neighbor's steps after a big snow. It means inevitable intimacy, a shared world of sidewalk games, gossip, hard-earned wisdom and home improvement tips reachable right from your porch.

When the Founding Fathers gathered at Independence Hall to conjure up the country they wanted to live in, they may not have envisioned some of the best things about this city today, particularly the multicultural population and the rich realms of art, music, food and more that such diversity has brought. But alongside the birth of the American experiment, there began a uniquely Philadelphian experiment in toughness and resilience, loyalty and pride. In this city, the talk is straight, your favorite cheesesteak spot is worth fighting for, and there's a reason the Flyers named their wild-eyed orange mascot Gritty. Not a bad blueprint for a place to call home. —The Editors

ESSENTIALS

TRANSPORT

BUS/RAIL
SEPTA
septa.org

BIKE SHARE
Indego
rideindego.com

LANDMARKS
INDEPENDENCE HALL
520 Chestnut St
Signing spot for America's
founding documents.

PHILADELPHIA MUSEUM OF ART
2600 Benjamin Franklin Pkwy
Paintings, sculpture and furniture, plus iconic steps.

EASTERN STATE PENITENTIARY
2027 Fairmount Ave
Former prison's ruins with a
criminal justice reform story.

MEDIA

MAGAZINE
Philadelphia
Smart, conversational intel.

RADIO
WHYY
Daily call-ins on *Radio Times*.

LITERARY
Apiary
Fresh poetry and prose.

GREENSPACE

FAIRMOUNT PARK
Reservoir Dr
Sprawling landscape of wooded
trails, sports fields, public art
and historic buildings along the
Schuylkill River's banks.

FOODWAY

SOFT PRETZEL
Salted, slightly crispy outside,
soft within. Best handed off
warm in a paper bag from the
corner store.

CALENDAR

JAN - MAY
Mummers Parade
Philadelphia Flower Show
Philly Craft Beer Festival

JUN - AUG
Roots Picnic
Nuevofest
BlackStar Film Festival

SEP - DEC
Feria del Barrio
OutFest
Apple Butter Frolic
   [Harleysville]

BOOKS
☞ *A Prayer for the City*
   by Buzz Bissinger
☞ *Philadelphia Fire*
   by John Edgar Wideman
☞ *2 A.M. at the Cat's Pajamas*
   by Marie-Helene Bertino

FRIDAY
Magic Gardens meander
Dinner at Vetri Cucina
Friday Saturday Sunday nightcap

....

SATURDAY
Breakfast at High Street on Market
Shopping for streetwear and sneaks
        at P's and Q's
Tehina shake at Goldie
Rittenhouse people-watching

....

SUNDAY
Schuylkill River Trail jog
Water ice at Fred's
Barnes Foundation browsing

MEMENTOS

Four Grain American Whiskey, *Manatawny Still Works*, $40
Pro messenger bag, *R.E.Load*, $254
Gritty votive candle, *VIX Emporium*, $10

RECORD COLLECTION

Boyz II Men	*Cooleyhighharmony*
The Roots	*Illadelph Halflife*
Hall & Oates	*Bigger Than Both of Us*
Rufus Harley	*Courage: The Atlantic Recordings*
Bardo Pond	*Lapsed*
Mazarin	*We're Already There*
Jill Scott	*Who Is Jill Scott: Words and Sounds Vol. 1*
Three Times Dope	*Original Stylin'*
The Philadelphia Experiment	*The Philadelphia Experiment*
King Britt Presents Sylk 130	*When the Funk Hits the Fan*
Birdie Busch	*The Ways We Try*
The War on Drugs	*Lost in the Dream*
Meek Mill	*Championships*
Teddy Pendergrass	*Teddy*
Kurt Vile	*Waking on a Pretty Daze*

ESSENTIALS

LODGING

Lokal
139 N 3rd St
Sleek, apartment-style "invisible service" hotel in the heart of Old City.

....

Pod Philly
31 S 19th St
City's first micro-hotel. Streamlined rooms, taqueria, social spaces to share.

....

Wm. Mulherin's Sons
1355 N Front St
Converted whiskey factory preserves industrial details; Italian restaurant below.

The Deacon
1600 Christian St
Stylishly renovated church. Bright Bauhaus feel alongside original stained glass.

....

Fitler Club
24 S 24th St
Industrial-chic rooms grant guests member perks: pool, spa, Vetri restaurant.

....

Four Seasons
1 N 19th St
Sky-high glitz, epic views. Glass-walled elevator to grand 60th-floor lobby.

WELLNESS

Studio 24
Community-oriented space for affordable yoga, art exhibitions and events. *4522 Baltimore Ave*

....

Rittenhouse Spa & Club
Luxe facials and body treatments. Pampering, yes, but energizing and nourishing too. *210 W Rittenhouse Sq*

....

EverybodyFights
Feeding Philly's fighting spirit. Old-school boxing gym meets fancy fitness studio. *1900 Market St*

COFFEE

ReAnimator
Fishtown

....

La Colombe
Rittenhouse

....

Menagerie
Old City

....

Ox
Queen Village

....

Elixr
Center City

BOOKSTORES

Joseph Fox Bookshop
Rittenhouse

....

Harriet's Bookshop
Fishtown

....

Uncle Bobbie's Coffee & Books
Germantown

....

A Novel Idea
East Passyunk

....

Big Blue Marble
Mount Airy

ISSUES

Education	The city school district's student body and funding have shrunk steadily for decades. As the district fights to keep teachers and repair aging infrastructure, many parents have turned to parochial, charter and private schools or fled to suburbs. **EXPERT:** *Dale Mezzacappa, the Philadelphia Public School Notebook*
Incarceration	Philly has the highest incarceration rate of any large jurisdiction in the country, with vast racial disparities: People of color made up 91 percent of the city's jail population as of June 2020. **EXPERT:** *Assata Thomas, Institute for Community Justice, Philadelphia FIGHT*
Inequality	Despite cultural and economic diversity, racial tension and discrimination persist. The city's Black community, about 44 percent of the population, disproportionately bears the effects of pollution and other environmental threats. **EXPERT:** *Judith Levine, Temple University*
Poverty	Hulking wrecks of decaying warehouses across stretches of the city symbolize the massive deindustrialization to which the former "Workshop of the World" lost 25 percent of its population and a huge portion of its tax base after the 1950s. Today, the poverty rate is roughly 25 percent. **EXPERT:** *Sister Mary Scullion, Project H.O.M.E.*

STATISTICS

316 C	Pantone for Midnight Green, Eagles Jersey color
28,750	Pipes in Wanamaker Organ
24	Hours cheesesteak rivals Pat's and Geno's are open
46,800	Coins produced per minute at Philadelphia Mint
30	Gallons of paint required for the average mural
$3	Usual price of a Citywide Special [PBR and Jim Beam shot]

NEIGHBORHOODS

RITTENHOUSE

Mansions and luxury high-rises overlook the Square in Philly's toniest zip code. Visitors flock for the density of destination dining and upscale shopping.

LOCAL: *Friday Saturday Sunday, Boyds, Vernick Food & Drink*

....

OLD CITY

Bounty of riches from the dawn of American democracy includes Liberty Bell, Independence Hall and Elfreth's Alley.

LOCAL: *Fork, Franklin Fountain, Spruce Street Harbor Park*

....

SOUTH PHILLY

Historically Italian American but increasingly diverse, with busy corridors like Italian Market and East Passyunk Avenue.

LOCAL: *Hardena, Brewery ARS, South Philly Barbacoa*

....

FAIRMOUNT

Quiet residential streets border museum-lined Benjamin Franklin Parkway. Scenic Schuylkill River Trail draws runners and bikers.

LOCAL: *Boathouse Row, Sabrina's Café, Franklin Fountain*

WEST PHILADELPHIA

Sprawling, largely residential section west of the Schuylkill River encompasses University City, Baltimore Avenue bustle and a dynamic restaurant scene.

LOCAL: *Jezabel's Cafe, 48th Street Grille, Mina's World*

....

FISHTOWN

Vibrant home to buzzy restaurants, beer gardens, live-music venues and indie boutiques on the Delaware River.

LOCAL: *St. Oner's, Cake Life Bake Shop, Weckerly's*

....

MANAYUNK

Main Street's bars and boutiques give off a small-town vibe; Center City proximity [and more-reasonable rents] attracts recent college grads.

LOCAL: *Le Bus Bakery, Pitchers Pub, the Couch Tomato*

....

NORTHEAST PHILLY

A collection of smaller, working-class neighborhoods with a robust immigrant population.

LOCAL: *Shish-Kabob Palace, Nifty Fifty's, Picanha Brazilian Steakhouse*

309

○ MOUNT AIRY

NORTHEAST PHILLY ☞

○ GERMANTOWN

○ MANAYUNK

1

NORTH PHILADELPHIA ○

76

611

13

KENSINGTON ○

○ BREWERYTOWN

FISHTOWN ○

30

FAIRMOUNT ○

DELAWARE RIVER

○ WEST PHILADELPHIA

RITTENHOUSE ○

○ OLD CITY

WASHINGTON SQUARE WEST ○

13

○ KINGSESSING BELLA VISTA ○

○ QUEEN VILLAGE

POINT BREEZE ○

○ PASSYUNK

SOUTH PHILLY ○

95

676

76

SELECTED CONTENT

014–015 *Food & Drink*

CHEESESTEAK
SOUL FOOD
ISRAELI
MEXICAN
CITYWIDE SPECIAL

016–017 *Shopping*

ANTIQUES
COMICS
RECORDS
TEAM GEAR
HOME BAR

018–019 *Action*

BLACK HISTORY
OFF-ROADING
DANCE PARTIES
STREET ART
MACABRE

020–021 *Expertise*

ART CONSERVATION
FOODWAYS
HIP-HOP DJ
TATTOOS
ENVIRONMENT

MORE THAN 80 PICKS ☞

BESTS

A curated list of city favorites—classic and new—from bars and restaurants to shops and experiences, plus a handful of can't-miss experts

FOOD & DRINK

For more Italian cuisine,
see our map on page 52.

CANNOLI
Isgro Pastries
1009 Christian St
Bella Vista
Family-owned Italian bake shop. Hand-filling cannolis with a spoon since 1904.

....

CHEESESTEAK
Dalessandro's
600 Wendover St
Roxborough
Crusty roll heaped with juicy, finely sliced rib-eye. Do not underestimate the tangy power of Cheez Whiz.

....

MORE CHEESESTEAK
John's Roast Pork
14 Snyder Ave
South Philly
No-frills, family-run since 1930. Sharp, gooey provolone melts into 12 hearty ounces of tender meat.

ITALIAN
Vetri Cucina
1312 Spruce St
Washington Square West
Dinner as elegant multicourse theater. Handmade pastas—fazzoletti with duck, almond tortellini—are the stars.

....

WATER ICE
John's Water Ice
701 Christian St
Bella Vista
A Philly staple: Made with fresh fruit, a thirst-quenching, slushier-than-a-snow-cone treat.

....

SOUL FOOD
Warmdaddy's
New location coming
Hot wings, skillet mac and honey butter cornbread with a side of live R&B. Also: jazz brunch.

MEXICAN
Blue Corn
940 S 9th St
Bella Vista
Fresh tortillas, rich sauces, classic margs. Taste of Mexico City in Italian Market.

....

ISRAELI
Zahav
237 St James Pl
Society Hill
James Beard Award-winning hummus, hearth-baked pita and hardwood-smoked lamb shoulder.

....

DIVE BAR
Oscar's Tavern
1524 Sansom St
Center City
Red booths, paper menus. Cheers to cheap beer and crabby fries in the heart of town.

SANDWICH

Tommy DiNic's

*Reading Terminal
Market, Center City*

Pilgrimage-worthy
roast pork with pro-
volone and garlicky
broccoli rabe.

....

PIZZA

Pizzeria Beddia

*1313 N Lee St
Fishtown*

Platonic ideal of
pizza, lofty critics
and lay fans agree.

....

BRASSERIE

Parc

*227 S 18th St
Rittenhouse*

Summon Paris with
steak frites, sidewalk
people-watching.

....

PHO

Pho 75

*1122 Washington Ave F
South Philly*

Fragrant broth,
fresh herbs. No-fuss
cafeteria vibe.

....

BREWERY

Dock Street West

*701 S 50th St
Cedar Park*

Wood-fired pizzas
and craft brews in a
restored firehouse.

THAI

Kalaya Thai Kitchen

*764 S 9th St
Bella Vista*

Winning hearts with
tapioca dumplings
and crabmeat curry.

....

VEGAN

Vedge

*1221 Locust St
Washington Square West*

Veggies get top bill-
ing: rutabaga fondue,
turnip carbonara.

....

BAKERY

Cafetería y Panadería
Las Rosas

*1712 S 8th St
Passyunk*

Follow the waft of
pastelitos, cakes and
churros.

....

DINER

Sam's Morning
Glory Diner

*735 S 10th St
Bella Vista*

Frittatas, biscuits
and the sassiest spe-
cials page in town.

....

NEIGHBORHOOD BAR

Martha

*2113 E York St
Kensington*

Homey and hip with
an epic beer list.

LEBANESE

Suraya

*1528 Frankford Ave
Fishtown*

Fresh man'oushe, ke-
babs, turmeric rice.
Go for the garden or
chef's counter.

....

TASTING MENU

Laurel

*1617 E Passyunk Ave
Passyunk*

Stylish BYO serves
intricate French-
inspired dishes.

....

BRUNCH

Middle Child

*248 S 11th St
Washington Square West*

Deli-diner. Outra-
geous, fluffy-egged
breakfast sammies.

....

CITYWIDE SPECIAL

Bob & Barbara's

*1509 South St
Rittenhouse*

Divey birthplace of
the Jim Beam shot/
PBR chaser combo.

....

ETHIOPIAN

Abyssinia

*229 S 45th St
Spruce Hill*

Casual, filling, deli-
cious. Semi-hidden
cocktail bar upstairs.

SHOPPING

COOKWARE

Fante's Kitchen Shop

1006 S 9th St
South Philly

Chef fave for classics plus ravioli stamps, fusilli irons and mezzalunas. An Italian Market institution.

....

BEAUTY SUPPLY

Marsh + Mane

529 S 4th St
Queen Village

Jenea Robinson's serene shop offers products and advice for cleansing, curling and conditioning natural hair.

....

RECORDS

Brewerytown Beats

2710 W Girard Ave
Brewerytown

Consult owner Max for clutch recs on hard-to-find vinyl. Don't miss $1 racks.

DEPARTMENT STORE

Boyds

1818 Chestnut St
Rittenhouse

Fourth-gen family-run. Master tailor Sergio Martins can fit any suit to flatter.

....

ANTIQUES

Jinxed

1331 Frankford Ave
Fishtown

Treasures from an upholstered high-heel chair to Benjamin Franklin Bridge blueprint art.

....

HOUSEWARES

Yowie

716 S 4th St
Queen Village

Shannon Maldonado's gallery-esque shop spotlights local makers, including totes featuring Philly artists' designs.

COMICS

Amalgam Comics & Coffeehouse

2578 Frankford Ave
Kensington

Owner Ariell Johnson has crafted an inclusive "Amalga-Nation."

....

FLAGS

Humphry's Flag Company

238 Arch St
Old City

Flags of every type and size. Earning its stars and stripes in Philly since 1864.

....

INDUSTRIAL

The Rowland Company

4900 N 20th St
Logan

PA's oldest company began making shovels in 1732. Now covers transmission needs.

TEAM GEAR

Mitchell & Ness
1201 *Chestnut St*
Center City
Turn back time with
felt pennants and
throwback jerseys.

....

NEEDLEWORK

M. Finkel & Daughter
936 *Pine St*
Washington Square West
Antique samplers
and silk embroider-
ies, history included.

....

HARDWARE

Rittenhouse Hardware
2001 *Pine St # 2*
Rittenhouse
Expert DIYers offer
gear and advice in
well-stocked aisles.

....

PLANTS

Urban Jungle
1526 *E Passyunk Ave*
Passyunk
Green oasis packed
with plants that
thrive in city spaces.

....

FURNISHINGS

Minima
131 *N 3rd St*
Old City
Contemporary fur-
niture and lighting
for clean, intimate
living spaces.

STATIONERY

Omoi Zakka Shop
1608 *Pine St*
Rittenhouse
Japanese-inspired
goods for elevated
letter-writing.

....

TOYS

Tildie's Toy Box
1829 *E Passyunk Ave*
Passyunk
Plush critters,
rainbow puzzles and
creativity kits.

....

WELLNESS

Ritual Shoppe
2003 *Walnut St*
Rittenhouse
Chic spot for
candles, crystal
jewelry and Philly-
themed tarot.

....

HOME BAR

Art in the Age
116 *N 3rd St*
Old City
Sip local spirits while
browsing bitters,
flasks and glassware.

....

ARTISAN GOODS

Moon + Arrow
742 *S 4th St*
Queen Village
Fine furnishings,
apparel, apothecary.
Artist pop-ups too.

VINTAGE

Retrospect Vintage
508 *South St*
South Philly
Goodwill-owned
emporium carries
one-of-a-kind pieces.

....

SILVER

Niederkorn
Antique Silver
244 *S 22nd St*
Fitler Square
Tiny shop gleams
with sterling brooches
and candlesticks.

....

HOME GOODS

Cuttalossa
47 *N 2nd St*
Old City
Bright outpost
for hand-loomed
textiles.

....

SKINCARE

Sabbatical Beauty
1901 *S 9th St # 308*
South Philly
Lush, Korean-
inspired small-batch
serums and scrubs.

....

JEWELRY

Bario Neal
524 *S 5th St*
Queen Village
Ethically sourced
stones; custom and
heirloom designs.

ACTION

For maps of the Waterfront and Sports,
see pages 55 and 67.

COLONIAL HISTORY

Once Upon a Nation
6th and Race streets
Old City
Stationed at
benches, storytellers
bring forgotten bits
of history to life.
....

PRIVATE COLLECTION

Barnes Foundation
2025 Benjamin
Franklin Pkwy
Fairmount
Eclectic works from
Picasso paintings
to sculptures from
the Dogon people
of Mali.
....

CULTURAL FESTIVAL

Odunde
odundefestival.org
Sprawling African
marketplace, perfor-
mances, Caribbean
food and procession
to Schuylkill River
each June.

CINEMA

PFS Roxy Theater
2023 Sansom St
Center City
Historic theater
screens first-run
indies and hosts
Philadelphia Film
Society's festival.
....

JAZZ

Ars Nova Workshop
arsnovaworkshop.org
Boundary-pushing
avant-garde jazz,
often in unconven-
tional spaces.
....

BLACK HISTORY

The Colored Girls
Museum
4613 Newhall St
Germantown
Artist-curated
"memoir museum"
in a converted Vic-
torian explores
the experiences of
women of color.

FARMERS MARKET

Clark Park Farmers'
Market
4300-4398 Baltimore
Ave, University City
Vast produce variety,
friendly vendors,
low-key West Philly
neighborhood vibes.
....

OFF-ROADING

Ready to Ride
Egg Harbor Town-
ship, NJ
Ride dirt bikes and
ATVs [illegal on
Philly streets] on
8 miles of woodsy
trails.
....

VARIETY SHOW

Tattooed Mom
530 South St
Queen Village
"You Can't Fail"
showcases art-in-
progress: spoken
word, stand-up,
painting, ballet.

STREET ART

Mural Mile
Walking Tour
muralarts.org
Wander Center City
and learn about
Philly's vibrant
outdoor art.

....

DANCE PARTIES

Warehouse on Watts
923 N Watts St
West Poplar
DJ sets and shows
with crisp sound and
cheap-ish drinks.

....

ARTIST COLLECTIVE

Vox Populi
319 N 11th St, 3rd fl
Callowhill
Talks, performances
and exhibitions of
experimental work.

....

RUMBA

iMPeRFeCT Gallery
5539 Germantown Ave
Germantown
Energetic Friday
night drumming,
singing and dancing.

....

RACE

Rocky 50k Fat
Ass Run
rocky50k.com
Unsanctioned run
traces Rocky's epic,
unlikely route.

PUPPETRY

Spiral Q
spiralq.org
Thought-provoking
performances for
kids and adults.

....

MACABRE

Mütter Museum
19 S 22nd St
Center City
Medical specimens
and oddities, weird
and wondrous.

....

SKATING RINK

Blue Cross RiverRink
101 S Christopher
Columbus Blvd
Old City
Lace up your skates:
ice in winter, roller
in summer.

....

CERAMICS

The Clay Studio
137-139 N 2nd St
Old City
Local-made pottery
and classes to craft
your own.

....

NATURE

John Heinz National
Wildlife Refuge
8601 Lindbergh Blvd
Tinnicum
Peaceful, marshy
trails. Look out for
migratory birds.

MUSIC VENUE

Johnny Brenda's
1201 Frankford Ave
Fishtown
Gastropub with
intimate indie rock
shows upstairs.

....

FIELD TRIP

Valley Forge
King of Prussia, PA
Rolling hills, ranger
walks and cannon-
firing demos.

....

AXE-THROWING

Urban Axes
2019 E Boston St
Kensington
Land bull's-eyes at
the country's first
ax-throwing club.
BYOB if you dare.

....

HIDDEN ART

Dirty Frank's
347 S 13th St
Washington Square West
Off the Wall gallery
inside eclectic bar.
Outside: Famous
Franks mural.

....

DRAG

Martha Graham
Cracker Cabaret
@TheMarthaMan
Raucous shows feature
mashups from Black
Sabbath to Lady Gaga.

EXPERTISE

POET LAUREATE

Trapeta B. Mayson

trapetamayson.com

Liberia-born writer and social worker. Her potent poems address immigration and mental health.

....

FOOD CRITIC

Craig LaBan

@CraigLaBan

Old-school yet open-minded *Philadelphia Inquirer* critic and columnist. Highest restaurant rating: four "bells."

....

FILMMAKING

Louis Massiah

scribe.org

Social justice-oriented documentarian and founder of Scribe Video Center, hub for media instruction and cultivation.

ART CONSERVATION

Sally Malenka

philamuseum.org

Philadelphia Museum of Art's conservator of decorative arts and sculpture. Advises the city on public art projects.

....

INTERVIEWS

Terry Gross

freshair.npr.org

Studious and empathetic host of WHYY's *Fresh Air* since 1975. Master of intimate conversation.

....

PUBLIC HEALTH

Dr. John Rich

drexel.edu

MacArthur-winning authority on the health care gaps and needs of Black men in urban spaces.

MONUMENTS

Paul M. Farber

@paul_farber

Curator, historian and co-founder of Monument Lab. Exploring and inter-rogating cultural memory.

....

FOODWAYS

Omar Tate

honeysucklephl.com

Writer and chef's pop-up Honeysuckle explores Black American heritage through food. Permanent space in the works.

....

LATINX DIASPORA

Dr. Carmen Febo San Miguel

tallerpr.org

Directs Taller Puertorriqueño, Philly's biggest org promoting Latinx arts and culture.

HIP-HOP DJ

DJ Bran

djbran.com

SoundCloud rapper, Hip-Hop 103.9 on-air personality and Meek Mill's tour DJ.

....

COLONIAL PHILADELPHIA

Jessica Roney

liberalarts.temple.edu

Studies Philly's role in the American Revolution.

....

ENVIRONMENT

Mike Weilbacher

@SCEEMike

Longtime enviro educator directs Schuylkill Center on the river's banks.

....

RECIDIVISM

People's Paper Co-op

peoplespaperco-op .weebly.com

Arts and advocacy programs to help women with reentry.

....

MUSIC ENSEMBLE

Thee Phantom & the Illharmonic Orchestra

theephantomhiphop.com

Beethoven meets breakbeats: hip-hop with orchestral accompaniment.

LIT SCENE

Blue Stoop

bluestoop.org

Building bookish community with scrappiness that matches the city's.

....

COMMUNITY ORGANIZER

Tommy Joshua

phillypeacepark.org

Co-founder of North Philly Peace Park, community garden and gathering space.

....

TATTOOS

Robert Kraiza

@rkraiza

Elaborate work for Crown and Feather Tattoo reflects illustration background.

....

ARCHITECT

Wesley Wei

wweiarchitects.com

Modern designs use natural materials to honor the bones of old buildings.

....

FURNITURE

Walt Wynne and Wai-Jee Ho

wwwoodworking.com

Sleekly designed, midcentury-inspired pieces.

STREET ART

Conrad Benner

streetsdept.com

Photoblog *Streets Dept* captures art across public spaces.

....

RUNNING

Jon Lyons

run215.com

Founder of Run215, network for Philly's running crews.

....

SPORTS COLUMNIST

Mike Sielski

@MikeSielski

Raised just outside Philly, named top U.S. sports writer by the AP in 2015.

....

UPCYCLED ART

RAIR

7333 Milnor St Northeast Philly

Nonprofit at a recycling plant challenges waste culture through artwork.

....

WOOD

Center for Art in Wood

141 N 3rd St Old City

Highlights artists working in wood, from everyday objects to sculpture.

SELECTED CONTENT

025 *Liberty Bell reviews*

026 *Workshop of the World*

028 *Sandwiches*

031 *Architecture of Note*

032 *William Penn's towering hat*

035 *Frank Rizzo's misdeeds*

036 *Row house games*

038 *Sports heartbreaks*

039 *Local Lexicon*

042 *Marian Anderson*

045 *Medical oddities*

046 *Lenapehoking*

048 *Dr. J*

049 *An elegy for MOVE*

MORE THAN 30 ENTRIES ▷

ALMANAC

A deep dive into the cultural heritage of
Philadelphia through news clippings, timelines, recipes,
reviews and other historical hearsay

THE JUNTO

In 1727, long before he became one of the nation's Founding Fathers, Benjamin Franklin founded the Junto, also known as the Leather Apron Club, in Philadelphia. The group gathered to discuss philosophical questions for mutual improvement. Original members included a shoemaker, a mathematician, a merchant, a cabinetmaker, a cobbler and an astrologer. Below, some of the questions Franklin used to lead discussions.

What new story have you lately heard agreeable for telling in conversation?

Hath any citizen in your knowledge failed in his business lately, and what have you heard of the cause?

Have you lately heard of any citizen's thriving well, and by what means?

What unhappy effects of intemperance have you lately observed or heard? of imprudence? of passion? or of any other vice or folly?

What happy effects of temperance? of prudence? of moderation? or of any other virtue?

Do you think of any thing at present, in which the Junto may be serviceable to mankind? to their country, to their friends, or to themselves?

Do you know of any deserving young beginner lately set up, whom it lies in the power of the Junto any way to encourage?

Have you lately observed any encroachment on the just liberties of the people?

Hath any body attacked your reputation lately? and what can the Junto do towards securing it?

Is there any man whose friendship you want, and which the Junto or any of them, can procure for you?

Have you lately heard any member's character attacked, and how have you defended it?

Have you any weighty affair in hand, in which you think the advice of the Junto may be of service?

— Excerpted from Benjamin Franklin's papers, 1728

ONE-STAR REVIEWS FOR THE LIBERTY BELL

Though most visitors find the storied bell worth seeing, some of those who walked away disappointed have taken their ire to Google or Tripadvisor.

Cracked bell behind glass ... better view in your history book, better mystique too. Go see South Philly instead!

....

Security is frustrating and pointless. It's a bell. Meanwhile, you can walk right up to Franklin's grave.

....

Having read the apparently rather informative boards relating to the bell I am still none the wiser as to why on earth this bell is significant in any way, shape or form. It seems to have no relevance to anything other than it tolled a few times and some historical figures may [or may not] have responded? And it was in the Independence Hall when the Declaration was signed? So what? It's a [flawed and poorly made] bell.

....

The Constitution needs to be rewritten. PERIOD.

....

I saw it from a window 'cause everything closes there at 5. So inconvenient. Our freedom isn't even free.

Boring. Long lines for a broken bell. Either fix the damn thing or get a new one. Nobody can explain why this is important. They just keep saying it's an institution of American independence, just like Cher. Don't see this if you wouldn't pay for a Cher concert.

....

I wasn't even allowed to ring it. Also it's not always sunny in Philadelphia.

....

Although the bell clearly has some level of importance in American history, I was completely disappointed with the way the bell had clearly been poorly kept through the years with a huge crack in it now. If I were running it I'd change the bell for something more modern like a jukebox, which will be able to provide far more entertaining sounds than that of a broken bell.

....

It is very clearly a fake.

....

Just a bell.

....

Salty.

WORKSHOP OF THE WORLD

*Textile mills, paper mills, glassworks, breweries, leather makers,
bookbinders, steelmakers, silk manufacturers, umbrella makers, sugar
refineries, hosiery companies, boot and shoe manufacturers, shipbuilders,
chemical and oil companies: Throughout the 19th and early 20th century,
thousands of companies employed tens of thousands of Philadelphians.
Below, a selection of notable items manufactured in Philly.*

Blaisdell paper pencils

Federal Pretzel Baking Company
soft pretzels

A.J. Reach baseball gloves

Wirt & Knox Manufacturing
Co.'s hoses and reels

John B. Stetson hats

Breyers ice cream

Atwater Kent Manufacturing
Company radios

Peeps candy

Budd Company railroad cars

Tastykakes

Philadelphia Coke Company
[fuel derived from coal for
smelting steel]

Rose Manufacturing Co. lamps

Cunningham pianos

Ford, Studebaker, Packard
and Cadillac cars

Peter Stretch clocks

F. S. Walton Co.'s neat's-foot
and lard oil

Keystone Dry Plates [for
photographs]

Doughboy's iron lids

Fretz, Gross, & Company
factory umbrellas and parasols

Campbell Soup Company soups

George W. Blabon Company Oil
Cloth and Linoleum Works

Disston and Sons saws

United States Gypsum Co.
gypsum wallboards and blocks

Nabisco cookies

S.L. Allen & Co.'s Flexible
Flyer sled

GERMANTOWN FRIENDS' PROTEST AGAINST SLAVERY

On behalf of the Germantown Monthly Meeting of the Religious Society of Friends, four men penned the first written protest against slavery in colonial America in 1688. Below, an excerpt.

There is a saying, that we shall doe to all men like as we will be done ourselves; making no difference of what generation, descent or colour they are. And those who steal or robb men, and those who buy or purchase them, are they not all alike? Here is liberty of conscience, wch is right and reasonable; here ought to be likewise liberty of ye body, except of evil-doers, wch is an other case. But to bring men hither, or to rob and sell them against their will, we stand against. In Europe there are many oppressed for conscience sake; and here there are those oppressed who are of a black colour. And we who know that men must not committ adultery—some do committ adultery, in others, separating wives from their husbands and giving them to others; and some sell the children of these poor creatures to other men. ... And we who profess that it is not lawful to steal, must, likewise, avoid to purchase such things as are stolen, but rather help to stop this robbing and stealing if possible. And such men ought to be delivered out of ye hands of ye robbers, and set free as well as in Europe. Then is Pennsylvania to have a good report, instead it hath now a bad one for this sake in other countries. Especially whereas ye Europeans are desirous to know in what manner ye Quakers doe rule in their province—and most of them doe look upon us with an envious eye. But if this is done well, what shall we say is done evil?

WILLIAM SAVERY

Philadelphia was the center of furniture making in the Colonies before the Revolution. William Savery worked on Second Street, where, like many joiners [as cabinetmakers were often called], he hung the "sign of the chair" at his door so customers could find him. Like many craftsmen of the 18th century, Savery did not inscribe all his pieces. Some bore the letter S, while others were labeled with "All sorts of Chairs and Joiners Work Made and Sold by WILLIAM SAVERY, At the Sign of the Chair, a little below the Market, in Second Street PHILADELPHIA." Benjamin Franklin was among Savery's patrons, and the Franklin family still owns a few of his pieces. A selection of Savery's Queen Anne-style chairs remains on display in the Governor's Council Chamber at Independence Hall.

SANDWICHES

Cheesesteak	Frizzled and fried beefsteak with cheese [locals choose Whiz, American or sometimes provolone] on a hoagie roll. Order it "wit" to add fried onions. *Pat's King of Steaks*
Roast Pork	Tender folds of hot, slow-roasted pork get a punch from sharp provolone and garlicky broccoli rabe or sautéed spinach. *John's Roast Pork*
Italian Hoagie	Sliced-to-order Italian deli meats like prosciutto, mortadella and soppressata layered with provolone or mozzarella [or both], plus shaved lettuce, tomatoes, pickles and seasonings, on a long hoagie roll. *Campo's Deli*
The So Long Sal!	Italian hoagie modernized with spicy lemon-artichoke spread and herb- and pepper-infused Duke's mayo, plus vinaigrette-dressed onions and arugula on a seeded Sarcone's roll. *Middle Child*
The PFD	Sarcone's roll, fried-to-order breaded chicken cutlet, fresh mozzarella, artichoke and prosciutto, drizzled with arugula pesto and balsamic glaze. *Angelo's Pizzeria*
The Forager	Breakfast sandwich with braised kale, seared king oyster mushrooms, Swiss and a runny fried egg on a house-made poppy seed roll. *High Street on Market*
Tuna Hoagie	Part of a nightly clandestine hoagie omakase for deluxe tuna-and-sardine combo, topped with red onions, olive tapenade, tomatoes and crunchy parsley. *Pizzeria Beddia*
Bánh Mi	Hot, house-baked baguette brimming with grilled lemongrass pork, pickled daikon, fresh veggies, sliced jalapeños and a fistful of cilantro at a decades-old classic Vietnamese bakery. *Ba Le Bakery*
Falafel	Crispy, perfectly spiced chickpea fritters and crunchy salad tucked into a soft, made-from-scratch pita and doused in creamy tahini. *Goldie*
Mr. Joe's	From the family behind Italian bakery Termini's, a panini with prosciutto, fresh mozz, tomato and basil. Served with a gratis glass of wine, salad and dessert. *Mr. Joe's Cafe*

YELLOW JACKETS

"Frankford Tops Bears in Thrilling Fray"
The Philadelphia Inquirer
December 5, 1926

Blazing over the ebbing, dying minutes of a thrilling battle like some sirocco sweeping the desert, the Frankford Yellow Jackets yesterday snatched victory from defeat when they conquered the Chicago Bears before 15,000 shivering supporters at Shibe Park, 7 to 6. It was in the final quarter that the great offensive of both teams burst through the adamantine defense of the rivals, and packed fifteen minutes with such drama, thrills and wonder plays that the spectators warmed in the heat of their own emotions. Coming from behind like some great escadrille, the Jackets swept through the air to wing their way to victory, a triumph that sent them in the van of the Bruins, and may be the salvation of the Chamberlin clan when final honors and a professional crown are awarded. Outstanding as the hero of the encounter was a manikin in moleskins, a shrimp in armor, but a giant in war, and his name is Homan. "Two Bits" they call this little warrior in the affectionate vocabulary of the idolator, but to Frankford he looked like a million dollars yesterday, two minutes before the final whistle sounded the knell of the Illinois invaders. Standing behind the Bruins' goal line, forty-five yards away from where the massive Stockton was circling, a football dangling like some limp rag in his sturdy right fist. "Two Bits" reached into the air and plucked a voluptuous pass out of the arctic breezes to score the touchdown that made the enemies tied.

The Frankford Yellow Jackets were Philadelphia's first professional football team. In the early 1930s, the Great Depression brought heavy financial challenges to the team along with a slew of shutout losses. In 1933, the NFL gave the team's assets to Bert Bell and Lud Wray, who named their new team the Philadelphia Eagles, echoing FDR's New Deal symbol. Only one of the players from the Yellow Jackets' last season went on to become an Eagle.

PSFS Building

Fisher Fine Arts Library

Vanna Venturi House

Philadelphia Museum of Art

ARCHITECTURE OF NOTE

FISHER FINE ARTS LIBRARY [1890] Cathedral-like Victorian Gothic building in dark red sandstone, designed by Philadelphia architect Frank Furness. Grand four-story brick-and-terra-cotta main reading room lets light into the interior rooms surrounding it. *220 S 34th St*

....

PHILADELPHIA MUSEUM OF ART [1928] Sweeping U-shaped Greek Revival complex presides over the city from a terraced rise at the end of Benjamin Franklin Parkway. Detail work, including the style of the columns at the entrance, by Julian Abele, first Black student to graduate from UPenn's Department of Architecture. *1600 Benjamin Franklin Pkwy*

....

VANNA VENTURI HOUSE [1964] Robert Venturi designed this postmodern home in Chestnut Hill for his mother. Strikingly flat grayish-green façade, pitched roof, curved and diagonal walls. A unique staircase narrows as it climbs. *8330 Millman St*

....

ESHERICK HOUSE [1961] Just a block from the Vanna Venturi House but a world away, designed by Louis Kahn. Rectangular concrete-and-stucco house with a flat roof; unusual geometric window configuration lets in lots of light. *204 Sunrise Ln*

....

PSFS BUILDING [1932] William Lescaze and George Howe designed the country's first International-style skyscraper for the Philadelphia Saving Fund Society. Though the bank itself was shut down in the 1990s—it's now the Loews Philadelphia Hotel—the iconic red neon "PSFS" sign still tops the 36-story building. *1200 Market St*

....

THE BARNES FOUNDATION [2012] Two sleek limestone buildings wrap around a sunny court, conceived by Tod Williams and Billie Tsien as a "a gallery in a garden and a garden in a gallery." The interior mirrors the gallery configuration at the original Barnes Foundation location in the suburbs. *2025 Benjamin Franklin Pkwy*

....

CIRA CENTRE [2005] Curtain wall skyscraper, immensely Instagrammable thanks to the flawless sky reflections off its smooth silver glass. Dynamic angular design makes the shape appear different from each direction. LED lights in shadowboxes create patterns behind the glass. *1929 Arch St*

WILLIAM PENN'S HAT

A 37-foot bronze statue of William Penn, founder of both the Province of Pennsylvania colony and the city of Philadelphia, stands atop City Hall. Measuring 548 feet high, including the statue, Philadelphia City Hall was the tallest habitable building in the world from its completion in 1894 until 1908. It remained the tallest in Philadelphia until 1986, thanks to a gentlemen's agreement that no building in the city should rise higher than Penn's hat. "I'm waving to Billy Penn right now," crane operator Charles McCue reported via radio on September 10, 1986, as he installed the first steel column of the 44th floor of the One Liberty Place skyscraper and made history, according to *The Philadelphia Inquirer*. Many Philadelphians believe the breaking of the agreement brought a curse upon Philly's pro sports teams. The supposed curse was lifted when the Phillies won the 2008 World Series.

SISTER ROSETTA THARPE

Tharpe is considered by many to be the godmother of rock and roll. Below, an account of the stir caused when she began fusing gospel with more popular, secular sounds.

"Sister Rosetta Tharpe Defends Gospel-Pop Fad"
The Philadelphia Tribune
July 6, 1963

The controversial "hot gospel show" now being featured at the Uptown is an extension of a new music craze which is sweeping plush night clubs from coast to coast. It is referred to on Tin Pan Alley as "Gospel Pop." The exploitation of Negro spirituals and gospel songs by night clubs and recording companies has been strongly criticized by many leading ministers. Last week, Mahalia Jackson, undisputed "queen" of the gospel singers, condemned entertainers who sing "gospel-pop" saying it is like "spitting in God's face." But, Sister Rosetta Tharpe, another famous gospel singer, defended the new fad when she appeared at the Underground last week. Said she: "Sinners go into night clubs and gospel people should go there to save them."

ITALIAN MARKET

The South 9th Street Curb Market is a sprawling tangle of shops, carts and specialty purveyors. Though best known for its Italian roots, the market has gathered a diverse mix of sellers and clientele since its inception.

1847..... St. Paul's Catholic church opens, welcoming Italian and Irish worshippers.

1854..... Pennsylvania's Act of Consolidation expands the official city limits, including South Philadelphia for the first time.

1884..... Antonio Palumbo opens a boarding house. Businesses like butchers, pastry shops and grocery stores spring up to serve the increasing Italian immigrant population.

1904..... Mario and Crucificia Isgro open Isgro Pastries. The family-run shop still sells Italian cookies, all-butter pound cakes and filled-to-order cannolis.

1930..... Brothers Pat and Harry Olivieri open a hot dog stall. Three years later, they make the first cheesesteak and eventually open Pat's King of Steaks.

1939..... Danny and Joe Di Bruno open a small grocery store. In 1965, inspired by a trip to Switzerland, the brothers reinvent the shop as Di Bruno Bros. "The House of Cheese."

1966..... Geno's Cheesesteaks opens across the street from Pat's King of Steaks, and an ongoing rivalry is born.

1976..... Sylvester Stallone's Rocky runs through the market in a training scene. A produce vendor tosses him an orange as he jogs past.

2007..... A historical marker is installed at the corner of 9th and Christian streets, honoring the market as an iconic city landmark.

2014..... Cristina Martinez and Ben Miller launch a taco cart selling lamb barbacoa that takes nearly a day to make and sells out in hours. Two years later, they open South Philly Barbacoa.

2019..... Chutatip "Nok" Suntaranon opens Kalaya, named for her mother and showcasing the Southern Thai cuisine of her youth.

2020..... Prompted by protests calling for racial justice, a prominent mural depicting former police commissioner and mayor Frank Rizzo is painted over.

PARKING PROBLEMS

In 1961, Philadelphia Mayor Richardson Dilworth proposed a parking plan that would require South Philadelphia residents to pay $3.50 per month to park on the street overnight. Below, an excerpt from The Philadelphia Inquirer's *account of what transpired on the night Dilworth announced the plan.*

"Rock Barrage Imperils Dilworth
As 2000 Protest His Parking Plan"
July 25, 1961

"Let's crash it!" That outcry from a group of 10 husky youths touched off the first show of violence outside the auditorium of the George Washington School, 5th and Federal sts., Monday night. It was 8:45. The youths, wearing undershirts or T-shirts in the warm, intermittent rain, stood on the lower step of a short flight of stairs leading to the auditorium. Behind them, elbow to elbow, stood a throng of more than 1000 vociferous, angry residents of South Philadelphia. For almost two hours the crowd had chanted its contempt for the Mayor's proposed pilot parking program. "No, no, no, no," the crowd chorused. "Down with Dilworth!" came the chant. The youth's outcry, and their sudden move up the stairs to make good their intention of "crashing" the already-packed auditorium, provided the spark. Three policemen standing at the top of the stairs leaped toward the doors. They swung them shut just as the youths reached the top, pressed on by the milling throng. That did it. A howl of outrage rose from the crowd. In an instant the air was full of beer cans, stones, bricks, tomatoes and peaches. … The barrage and the shouting went on. Then Police Inspector Denis Gealer emerged from the auditorium with three other officers. Gealer appealed for quiet—and the tumult died down. Then he folded his arms—like an Indian chief, of the movie and TV Westerns—and stood at the top of the stairs. He said nothing, but watched the crowd intently.

Parking in South Philly remains a fiery issue. People here seem to park wherever they please, including in the center lane of Broad Street, a century-old practice that is technically illegal. In 2017, a political action committee's lawsuit aimed at getting officials to enforce tickets for parking on the median was dismissed by a Common Pleas Court judge.

THE CRIMES OF FRANK RIZZO

*The former police commissioner and mayor is widely reviled for a legacy
of police brutality, political patronage and segregationist policies.*

1965 As deputy commissioner, Rizzo orders cops to attack 25 peaceful Black protesters demonstrating for integration at Girard College.

1967 Rizzo is appointed Philadelphia police commissioner. At a peaceful protest outside the Board of Education, Rizzo orders officers to attack a crowd of 3,000 primarily Black students.

1970 Rizzo orders a raid on the Philadelphia offices of the Black Panther Party. On August 31, police attack and strip-search the Panthers at gunpoint on the sidewalk.

1972-78 As mayor, Rizzo devotes more funds and better benefits to the police department than ever before and raises the city's wage tax from 3.3 to 4.3 percent.

1978 On August 8, after months of attempting to evict the African American activist group MOVE, police and activists exchange fire. One officer is killed.

1985 Rizzo is out of office when the police end a second confrontation with MOVE by bombing the group's new house on May 13, killing 11 people and causing a fire that destroys at least 61 homes.

1991 Rizzo dies of a heart attack while campaigning for a third mayoral term.

2020 Following weeks of protest over the death of George Floyd, a monument to Rizzo in front of the Municipal Services Building is removed in the predawn hours of June 3.

TERRY GROSS

In Terry Gross' 45 years hosting WHYY's *Fresh Air*, her intimate interviews have become the gold standard. Reflecting on her career in 2018, she told *The New York Times*: "I read, watch or listen to as much of the person's work as possible, so I have an understanding of what makes them, or their story, important." On her trademark probing: "I tell people that if I ask them anything too personal they should let me know and I'll move on." Best conversation opener? "Tell me about yourself."

ROW HOUSE SPORTS

In the days before air conditioning and the internet, young Philadelphians played numerous street games of varying levels of complexity and safety. One of the most popular was deadbox, which typically involved tossing bottle caps into a chalk-drawn grid. A selection of other once-popular street games:

TINNY TINNY TIN CAN	KICK THE WICKEY
BUCK BUCK	WALL BALL
HALF-BALL	WIRE BALL
KICK THE CAN	STEP BALL
CHINK	BOX BALL
STICK BALL	HIDE THE BELT
HOSE BALL	DIAMOND BALL

W.E.B. DU BOIS

In 1896, activist and scholar W.E.B. Du Bois came to Philadelphia to study the socioeconomic conditions of the city's Black population. His research provided the foundation for the first sociological study of Black life in America, The Philadelphia Negro. *Below, an excerpt.*

In Philadelphia, as elsewhere in the United States, the existence of certain peculiar social problems affecting the Negro people are plainly manifest. Here is a large group of people perhaps forty-five thousand, a city within a city—who do not form an integral part of the larger social group. This in itself is not altogether unusual ... and yet in the case of the Negroes the segregation is more conspicuous, more patent to the eye, and so intertwined with a long historic evolution, with peculiarly pressing social problems of poverty, ignorance, crime and labor, that the Negro problem far surpasses in scientific interest and social gravity most of the other race or class questions. ... What, then, of this great mass of the population? Manifestly they form a class with social problems of their own—the problems of the Thirtieth Ward differ from the problems of the Fifth, as the black inhabitants differ. In the former ward we have represented the rank and file of Negro working-people; laborers and servants, porters and waiters. This is at present the great middle class of Negroes feeding the slums on the one hand and the upper class on the other. Here are social questions and conditions which must receive the most careful attention and patient interpretation.

BENJAMIN FRANKLIN PARKWAY

Philadelphia's key cultural institutions line the grand diagonal boule-vard—originally called Fairmount Parkway—that connects Center City to Fairmount Park. To make way for its construction, at least 1,300 structures were demolished. The Philadelphia Inquirer *recounted the ceremonial removal of the first brick.*

"Parkway Started by Razing of First Building"
February 23, 1907

It was an old-fashioned dwelling, just in the shape it had been when the tenants moved out. The party, headed by Director Hathaway, entered the house and one by one up a rickety ladder climbed to the roof. There, just as the clock struck 12, the Director raised his silver pick and began loosening a brick on the chimney. Several hundred persons on the street below gave a cheer as the first brick was pecked out and held aloft. It was a hazardous ceremony, even if it was simple. It was no easy task to climb to the roof. The house was rickety, the ladder shaky and the wind blowing. The party did not tarry after the first brick was out.

When they reached the ground the party adjourned to a nearby restaurant, where luncheon was served. Here Councilman John W. Ford, in a brief speech, presented to the Director the silver pick with which the first brick had been loosened. The pick had been padded in a satin-lined case and was inscribed: "Presented to John R. Hathaway, Director of Public Works, at the beginning of the operation on the Parkway, February 22, 1907, by Howard E. Ruch, contractor." In accepting the souvenir the Director said: "I regard this as an era in Philadelphia's history, and I shall cherish this souvenir to my dying day."

For deep history of the parkway, read Building the City Beautiful: The Benjamin Franklin Parkway and the Philadelphia Museum of Art *by David B. Brownlee. Brownlee is a historian of modern architecture and professor of art history at the University of Pennsylvania. First published in 1989, an updated edition was released in 2017 for the parkway's centennial.*

NEAR MISSES

In the world of Philly sports, there is a storied history of getting very close to winning it all but coming up short. Fans are accustomed to broken hearts—and eternal hope.

76ERS VS. LAKERS [2001]

A scrappy 76ers team, spurred by the mercurial Allen Iverson's dynamic play, faced off with the star-studded Lakers in the 2001 NBA Finals. Shockingly, the underdog Sixers managed to snatch the first game from the purple-and-gold. But after that initial high, Philadelphia bowed under the brute force of center Shaquille O'Neal, dropping four consecutive games to lose the series.

EAGLES VS. PATRIOTS [2004]

In the early 2000s, the Eagles made it to the NFC championship game three years in a row, and every year their luck ran out before the Super Bowl. In 2004, when the Birds finally made it to the big game, they turned in a turgid performance in a loss to the New England Patriots, leaving Eagles fans brokenhearted once again.

PHILLIES VS. BLUE JAYS [1993]

The 1993 Phillies, a colorful cast of characters who captured the heart of the city, made it all the way to the World Series. But in a decisive Game 6, Toronto Blue Jays catcher Joe Carter hit a game-winning homer off Mitch "Wild Thing" Williams and ensured Philadelphia's wait for championship glory would stretch on for another year—or 15.

FLYERS VS. BLACKHAWKS [2010]

The closest the Flyers have come to winning a championship since the late 1970s came in 2010, when they faced the Chicago Blackhawks in the Stanley Cup Finals. The Flyers looked capable of pushing the Blackhawks to a winner-take-all Game 7 but fell just short as Chicago managed to score an overtime goal in Game 6, ending the series and continuing the Flyers' title drought.

JOE FRAZIER VS. MUHAMMAD ALI [1975]

"Smokin'" Joe Frazier evoked the quiet toughness and never-say-die attitude that Philadelphians hold so dear. When he and the legendary Ali squared off in the Thrilla in Manila, one of boxing's most celebrated fights, the epic bout left both men broken and forever changed. Though Ali came out on top, Frazier lamented, "Man, I hit him with punches that'd bring down the walls of a city."

KENSINGTON

Though deindustrialization has since vastly changed the neighborhood, in the 19th century, Kensington was a working-class hub of factories and textile mills.

What can be said of the Kensington of today, with her long line of business streets, her palatial residences and beautiful homes, that we do not know?

A City within a City, nestling upon the bosom of the placid Delaware. Filled to the brim with enterprise, dotted with factories so numerous that the rising smoke obscures the sky. The hum of industry is heard in every corner of its broad expanse. A happy and contented people, enjoying plenty in a land of plenty.

Populated by brave men, fair women and a hardy generation of young blood that will take the reins when the fathers have passed away. All hail, Kensington! A credit to the Continent—a crowning glory to the City.

—Kensington: A City Within a City, 1891

LOCAL LEXICON

YOUSE
Philly's "y'all" equivalent.

....

JAWN
Pretty much any person, place, thing, depending on context.

....

BOL
Boy. Often "young bol," addressing someone younger than the speaker. Sometimes spelled "boul" or "bull."

....

OCKY
Fake or inauthentic, often referring to imitation brand-name clothes.

WIT/WID
"With," as in you want your cheesesteak with onions. No onions? "Widdout."

....

WHIZ
What to say when ordering your cheesesteak with the processed cheese product known as Cheez Whiz. Cheese and onions? "Whiz wit."

....

WATER ICE
Fruit, sugar and ice in a cup. Firmer than a slushy, softer than shaved ice. Pronounced "wooder ice."

CORRUPTION

In July 1903, journalist Lincoln Steffens published "Philadelphia: Corrupt and Contented," one in a series of articles exposing municipal corruption in the U.S. Below, an excerpt.

Other American cities, no matter how bad their own condition may be, all point with scorn to Philadelphia as worse—the worst-governed city in the country. St. Louis, Minneapolis, Pittsburg submit with some patience to the jibes of any other community; the most friendly suggestion from Philadelphia is rejected with contempt. The Philadelphians are "supine," "asleep"; hopelessly ring-ruled, they are "complacent." ... Philadelphia is one of the oldest of our cities and treasures for us scenes and relics of some of the noblest traditions of "our fair land." Yet I was told how once, "for a joke," a party of boodlers counted out the "divvy" of their graft in unison with the ancient chime of Independence Hall. ... All our municipal governments are more or less bad, and all our people are optimists. Philadelphia is simply the most corrupt and the most contented. ... Philadelphia is proud; good people there defend corruption and boast of their machine. My college professor, with his philosophic view of "rake-offs," is one Philadelphia type. Another is the man, who, driven to bay with his local pride, says: "At least you must admit that our machine is the best you have ever seen."

EDMUND BACON

The executive director of the Philadelphia City Planning Commission from 1949 to 1970, Edmund Bacon [father of actor Kevin] became known as the "Father of Modern Philadelphia." Below, highlights from the architect and urban planner's eight foundational Elements of Involvement.

MEETING THE SKY	A skyline should be a major determinant in city building.
MEETING THE GROUND	The way a building rises from the earth determines the structure's quality.
ASCENT AND DESCENT	Use of varying levels to produce anticipation and satisfaction.
CONVEXITY AND CONCAVITY	How forms envelop and involve us in their spatial animation.
RELATIONSHIP TO MAN	How forms are carefully scaled to involve the people within the building.

THE PEOPLE'S PHILADELPHIA COOKBOOK

*In 1976, a grassroots organization then called the People's Fund
[it became the Bread & Roses Community Fund] published
a cookbook and sold copies for $5 to raise money for social and
economic justice causes. Below, a recipe from the cookbook.*

RESISTANCE PRINT SHOP SANDWICH NO. 2

*[During the crucial year of 1973–74, these sandwiches kept us going
at the shop. They aren't extravagant, but they're tasty.]*

Serves 2

2 eggs

blob of butter, oil or margarine

1 chopped onion

2-3 oz. grated cheese

2 or 4 slices bread [open or closed faced]

mayonnaise

salt and basil

mittens

Heat a frying pan [preferably dirty] and brown the onions in the
blob. Sprinkle with basil and salt. Crack the eggs over the onions
and sprinkle with the cheese.

Cook until egg is set, but not done. Then lift the egg and onions
out of the pan somehow and put one slice of bread under it. Put
the egg and onions back on the bread and put the second slice of
bread on top [for closed faces only]. Grill as you would any grilled
sandwich.

This meal was traditionally served with lots of mayonnaise at an
indoor temperature not above 32F and eaten with mittens.

—Reprinted by permission of Bread & Roses Community Fund

MARIAN ANDERSON

*Famed Black contralto Marian Anderson was born and raised in
Philadelphia. When the Daughters of the American Revolution denied her
a stage at Constitution Hall in 1939, first lady Eleanor Roosevelt resigned
from the organization in protest and helped arrange an alternative venue.*

"Throng Honors Marian Anderson In Concert at Lincoln Memorial"
The New York Times
April 10, 1939

An enthusiastic crowd estimated at 75,000, including many government officials, stood at the foot of Lincoln Memorial today and heard Marian Anderson, Negro contralto, give a concert and tendered her an unusual ovation. ... The audience, about half composed of Negroes, was gathered in a semi-circle at the foot of the great marble monument to the man who emancipated the Negroes. It stretched half-way around the long reflecting pool. Miss Anderson was applauded heartily after each of her numbers and was forced to give an encore.

When the concert was finished the crowd, in attempting to congratulate Miss Anderson, threatened to mob her and police had to rush her back inside the Memorial where the heroic statue of Lincoln towers. ... Secretary Ickes, who granted Miss Anderson permission to sing at this site, sat on her right on the monument's plaza, just above the specially arranged platform from which Miss Anderson sang into six microphones that carried the sound of her voice for blocks and over radio channels to millions throughout the country. ... Miss Anderson wore a tan fur coat with a bright orange and yellow scarf about her throat. She was bareheaded. Her mother was present.

In introducing Miss Anderson, Mr. Ickes referred to the Washington Monument at one end of the reflecting pool and to the Lincoln Memorial and in an implied rebuke to the D.A.R. remarked that "in our own time too many pay mere lip service to these twin planets in our democratic heaven."

"In this great auditorium under the sky all of us are free," the Secretary asserted. "When God gave us this wonderful outdoors and the sun, the moon and the stars, He made no distinction of race, creed, or color."

In a few brief remarks at the end of her concert Miss Anderson said: "I am so overwhelmed, I just can't talk. I can't tell you what you have done for me today. I thank you from the bottom of my heart again and again."

MUMMERS PARADE

Each New Year's Day, thousands of marchers flamboyantly costumed in sequins, satin and mylar participate in the Mummers Parade and compete for prizes. Though it borrows from English, Irish and Swedish traditions, the event is uniquely Philadelphian. The parade has grown more diverse in recent years, but it has a complicated [and often racist] history. The early history is hard to trace, but by the 1790s, George Washington was welcoming Philadelphians in costume to celebrate New Year's Day by going door to door, sharing jokes and poetry in exchange for drinks and cake. By the late 19th century, neighborhood groups had taken to parading in comic and fancy-dress clubs, a precursor to today's Mummers divisions: Fancy, Wench, Comic, String Band and Fancy Brigade. The first city-sponsored Mummers Parade took place in 1901. It incorporated aspects of minstrel shows—including performances in blackface, a specter that has followed the event into the present despite efforts to ban it. In 2020, after two marchers wore blackface in the parade, Councilwoman Cindy Bass introduced a bill to penalize the practice. "Every year, we have this conversation on Jan. 2; every year, they say it's going to be better, it's not going to happen again," Bass told *The New York Times*. "And it happens again."

ROCKY: TWO TAKES

THE HOLLYWOOD REPORTER   November 5, 1976

"The performances ... seem to respond to the originality and the sense of truth that underlies their characters. And a final word must be said for James Crabe's incredible camera work—not only his stunning views of Philadelphia's historic monuments, but the squalor of the South Philadelphia slums, two breath-taking swoops up the broad steps of the Philadelphia Art Museum, a protracted run past swinging sides of beef in a meat-packing plant and, of course, the virtuoso photography of the climactic bout. In many ways, *Rocky* is a picture that should make movie history." —*Arthur Knight*

....

THE NEW YORK TIMES   November 22, 1976

"Not since *The Great Gatsby* two years ago has any film come into town more absurdly oversold than *Rocky*, the sentimental little slum movie that opened yesterday at the Cinema II. ... Be warned." —*Vincent Canby*

ODDITIES OF NOTE

MAILLARDET'S AUTOMATON

The "Draughtsman-Writer" arrived at the Franklin Institute in 1928 in pieces. The boy-shaped brass machine was built by Swiss mechanician Henri Maillardet around 1800. Its "memory" includes four drawings and three poems, more than any other automaton. *The Franklin Institute*

GRIP THE RAVEN

Now taxidermied and mounted, Charles Dickens' one-time pet played a role in his 1841 serial novel *Barnaby Rudge*. When Edgar Allan Poe reviewed the book, he suggested the bird could have been "prophetically heard" in the story. Soon after, Poe published—you guessed it—"The Raven." *Free Library of Philadelphia*

OLD BALDY

Union General George Meade was best known for defeating Robert E. Lee in the 1863 Battle of Gettysburg. His horse, Old Baldy, was wounded multiple times but outlived Meade by 10 years. After Old Baldy was buried, two Union veterans disinterred him and sent his head to be taxidermied. *Grand Army of the Republic Museum & Library*

THE SOAP LADY

Exhumed in 1875, the woman's corpse had turned entirely into adipocere, a waxy, soap-like substance that can form from body fat after death in rare cases. X-rays revealed that the woman likely died in the 1830s or later and was between her late 20s and early 40s. *Mütter Museum*

HARRIET COLE'S NERVOUS SYSTEM

In 1888, a professor of anatomy at Hahnemann Medical College became the first person to extract a complete nervous system. The body belonged to Harriet Cole, a 35- to 40-year-old Black woman who died of tuberculosis and had done custodial work at the college. The process took more than five months. *Drexel University College of Medicine*

BUCKET OF TEETH

Dentist Edgar Randolf Rudolf Parker, who graduated from Philadelphia Dental College [now Temple's school of dentistry] in 1892, created a traveling dental circus. "Painless Parker" gathered crowds to his horse-drawn wagon and offered—with a wooden bucket of teeth at his feet to prove his mettle—to extract a rotten tooth pain-free for 50 cents. *Weaver Historical Dental Museum, Temple University's Kornberg School of Dentistry*

SANTA AND THE EAGLES

1968 was not a good year for the Philadelphia Eagles. On December 15, they entered their final game of the season—against the Minnesota Vikings—with a 2-11 record. Fans were agitated, and the weather was poor: 28 degrees with 20-mile-per-hour winds. And then the halftime Santa didn't show. Nineteen-year-old Frank Olivo, who had come to the game dressed in a Santa suit and beard, was asked to fill in. As he cheerily toured the stadium, fans pelted the substitute Santa with snowballs and boos, a now-legendary incident that contributed to the city's reputation for zealous and rowdy sports fandom. The Eagles lost the game.

LENAPEHOKING

*Before European settlers arrived and began to forcefully displace Native
American tribes, the Lenape inhabited an area they called Lenapehoking.
Their homeland covered much of what is now the mid-Atlantic states. Below,
a list of Philadelphia place names that reference the Lenape's legacy on this land.*

MANAYUNK (NEIGHBORHOOD AND CANAL)
"Place where we go to drink," referring to the Schuylkill River

PASSYUNK (NEIGHBORHOOD AND AVENUE)
Derived from *Pachsegink* or *Pachsegonk,* meaning "in the valley"
or "place between the hills"

KINGSESSING (NEIGHBORHOOD)
From *Chingsessing,* "a place where there is a meadow"

WISSAHICKON (CREEK, NEIGHBORHOOD)
From *Wisameckhan,* "catfish stream"

PENNYPACK (NEIGHBORHOOD, PARK, CREEK)
From *Pënëpèkw,* "downward-flowing water"

TULPEHOCKEN (RAIL STATION)
"Land of the turtles," referring to the Turtle Clan of the Lenape

PENNSYLVANIA PACKET

First published weekly in 1771, The Pennsylvania Packet and General Advertiser *became the country's first daily newspaper in* 1784. *Below, a selection of advertisements from the October* 28, 1771, *edition.*

GEORGE BARTRAM,

At the sign of the GOLDEN FLEECE'S HEAD, in Second-Street, between Cheftnut and Walnut Streets, HAS for Sale, at the moft reafonable Rates, for ready Money, a very large Quantity of SUPER, SUPER-FINE and COARSE BROADCLOTHS, of the beft Quality, and the moft faffionable Colours, from 40 s. To 7 s 6 d. per yard, with Rattinets, Shalloons and other Trimmings.

Juft imported, in the laft veffels from London, Liverpool and Hull, and to be fold on very low terms, by JOHN KAIGHN, At his Store, on the weft fide of Second-ftreet, between Market and Arch ftreets, two doors below the church, A NEAT and GENERAL ASSORTMENT of EUROPEAN and EAST INDIA GOODS, fuitable to the feafon; among which are, an affortment of SILVER WATCHES, neat FOWLING PIECES, and fine and coarfe three thread laid SEIN TWINE. Alfo, pickled Shad and Herrings in barrels. *N.B.* All perfons indebted to him above the ufual time of credit, are requefted to pay off their refpective accounts.

A BARREL ORGAN,

Made by GEO. PYKE, Maker to his Majefty,
Juft landed, and to be fold on very reafonable Terms, by
JOHN MURGATROYD,
In Water-Street, naer Tun-Alley;
The Tunes marked upon it are as follows;

CORONATION ANTHEM and ARIADNE;	Auretti's minuet,
Minuet by Weideman,	Hunting fong in Apollo,
Royal wedding,	Mrs. Vernon's hornpipe,
Lovely Nancy,	Handel's air,
Bellifle march,	Thro' the wood, laddie,
College hornpipe,	In infancy,
Handel's water piece,	Rule Britannia,
Chalk's hornpipe,	Cruel tyrant love,
Grane's march,	CIV. pfalm,
	Eafter Hymn.

JAZZ

"See 'Jazz' on Wane"
Evening Public Ledger
September 19, 1921

Philadelphia bands leaders have pronounced "jazz" music as tottering on its last legs before sinking into oblivion along with the other fads in music which have temporarily touched the fancy of the public and passed.

Cyrus E. Hummel, band leader, expressed the belief that the campaign of the last year against jazz music is responsible for a change in the taste of the public.

"It is true that people were jazz-mad a year ago. But now they will sit through programs that feature the compositions of Wagner, Liszt and Chopin, and will express dissatisfaction and leave if jazz music is played."

Joseph Kiefer, leader of the Philadelphia Police Band, sounded an appeal to musicians to refrain from "jazzing up" popular songs, waltzes and other dance numbers, but to adhere to the tempo mentioned in the scores.

DR. J

Everything about Julius Erving, both on and off the court, was larger-than-life. His massive hands could palm a basketball with ease, a prominent Afro topped his 6-foot-7 frame, and he could bound over other giants with ease. Erving, better known as Dr. J, came to Philadelphia in 1976, after he was traded from the New York Nets to the 76ers. The Doctor had already established himself as a star, but once he arrived in the City of Brotherly Love, his game and fame ascended to new heights, and he became, arguably, the greatest player in franchise history. He brought Philly its only championship of the last half-century when he took down the dynastic Los Angeles Lakers in 1983. Prior to his rise, 7-foot behemoths dominated the game through sheer size. But Erving, with his aerial capabilities and stylish play, showed a different way to stardom. The stars who came after him followed Erving's path: It's not a stretch to say that without Dr. J, there may never have been a Michael Jordan or a Kobe Bryant or a LeBron James.

THE MOVE BOMBING

On May 13, 1985, long-brewing tensions between the Philadelphia Police Department and the Black liberation group MOVE reached a horrific crescendo. After attempting to evict the group by force, police bombed the row house on Osage Avenue, in West Philadelphia, where MOVE members were living. The fire killed 11 people, five of them children, and destroyed 61 homes. Though it left only a vague imprint in our national cultural memory, the bombing and its reverberations deeply shook Philadelphians and changed the city forever. Poet Sonia Sanchez wrote "Elegy [for MOVE and Philadelphia]," an eight-part poem, shortly after the tragedy. Many years later, in 2011, Sanchez became Philadelphia's first poet laureate. Below, an excerpt.

beyond the mornings and afternoons
and deaths detonating the city.
beyond the tourist roadhouses
trading in lobotomies
there is a glimpse of earth
this prodigal earth.
beyond edicts and commandments
commissioned by puritans
there are people navigating the breath of hurricanes.
beyond concerts and football
and mummers strutting their
sequined processionals.
there is this earth. this country. this city.
this people.
collecting skeletons from waiting rooms
lying in wait. for honor and peace.
one day.

In the 2013 documentary Let the Fire Burn, *filmmaker Jason Osder uses archival footage to reconstruct the story of the bombing and the events surrounding it.*

INCLUDED

052-054   **BUON APPETITO**
           Eight institutions that reveal the range
           of Philly's Italian dining scene.

055-057   **WATERFRONT**
           Where to enjoy the city's two rivers, from trails
           to boathouses and ships.

058-060   **HIP-HOP**
           Relive the key moments of hip-hop history
           that unfolded in Philadelphia.

061-063   **PUBLIC ART**
           Pieces from the city's extensive collection
           of sculptures and murals open to all.

064-066   **BENJAMIN FRANKLIN**
           Highlights from the bounty of local sites linked
           to the Founding Father's legacy.

067-069   **SPORTS**
           Beyond the major league teams, find forgotten
           ball fields and legendary boxing gyms.

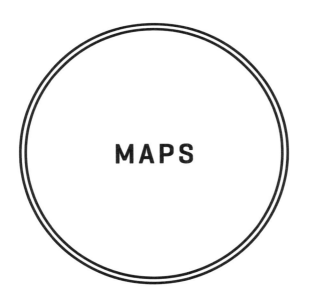

MAPS

———

Pictorial journeys through unique Philadelphia culture,
commerce and landscape by local illustrator Derick Jones.
Not to scale.

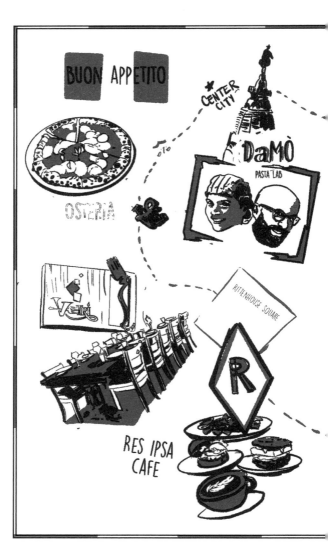

BELLA VISTA

fiore

Mr Martino's
tratt 12

PASSYUNK AVE

FILIPPO PALIZZI
CLUB

SOUTH PHILLY

Le Virtù

PALIZZI
SOCIAL
CLUB

BUON APPETITO

The Italian food scene runs deep, from red gravy joints and rustic regional cuisine to white-tablecloth fine-dining destinations.

VETRI CUCINA

Elegant, multicourse tasting menus showcasing Marc Vetri's epic handmade pastas in an intimate townhouse dining room. *1312 Spruce St*

LE VIRTÙ

Rustic restaurant specializing in fresh pastas and house-cured salumi. Hosts La Panarda, a lavish, 40-course feast, twice a year. *1927 E Passyunk Ave*

PALIZZI SOCIAL CLUB

When the red neon light flicks on, members flash cards to access the 100-year-old club's red gravy classics, cocktails in coupe glasses and old-school vibe. *1408 S 12th St*

FIORE FINE FOODS

Morning: fresh-baked flatbread egg sandwiches and pistachio cornetti. Dinnertime: handmade pastas and black tea–smoked duck. Sample from the robust amaro collection. *757 S Front St*

RES IPSA CAFE

Bustling coffee shop transforms into a cozy BYOB by night, showcasing chef Michael Vincent Ferreri's Southern Italian specialties. *2218 Walnut St*

MR. MARTINO'S TRATTORIA

Open three days a week and cash-only, the charming, family-run classic spot serves dishes like baked ricotta and veal tortellini. *1646 E Passyunk Ave*

DAMÒ PASTA LAB

An Italian-born couple feeds the Center City lunch crowd with paper bowls full of house-made Amatriciana, cacio e pepe and pesto pastas. *105 S 12th St*

OSTERIA

A modern iteration of the classic Italian taverna. Perfect pizza and pastas in a choice of settings: rustic dining room, intimate wine cellar or bright solarium. *640 N Broad St*

> LANGUAGE MATTERS *Italian Americans' preferred term for a hearty tomato-y pasta sauce differs from city to city [and sometimes neighborhood to neighborhood]. But Philly is decidedly a red gravy town.*

WATERFRONT

Verdant parks, pleasant trails and bits of reclaimed industrial history line the mighty Delaware and the skinnier Schuylkill.

PENN'S LANDING

Summer brings live music and community festivals along the Delaware River, plus beer gardens and hammocks in Spruce Street Harbor Park. In winter, ice skating. Stroll down Cherry Street Pier. *Front and Market Sts*

PENN TREATY PARK

In 1682, William Penn signed a treaty with the Lenape, which was honored during his lifetime. According to folklore, the parties signed under a giant elm tree in this small riverside park. *1301 N Beach St*

SCHUYLKILL RIVER TRAIL

Built mainly over abandoned rail lines, the trail runs all the way to Valley Forge. *Bridges on Walnut, Chestnut and Market Sts*

BARTRAM'S GARDEN

Lush greenery and peaceful trails surround this arboretum and botanical garden right off the Schuylkill. Historic house, community farm, plants for sale and free canoe rentals. *5400 Lindbergh Blvd*

SS UNITED STATES

This massive '50s luxury superliner broke speed records crossing the Atlantic. Today, it sits covered in rust on the Delaware River, awaiting restoration. *Pier 82*

WISSAHICKON VALLEY PARK

Walk or bike Forbidden Drive [no cars; the name's accurate] or steeper wooded trails. The once-secluded Devil's Pool may be too popular for its own good—check online before visiting, and leave no trace. *4900 Ridge Ave*

MANAYUNK TOWPATH

Walk along the canal, a tiny link in a historic chain of industrial waterways used to transport commodities like coal by barge. Look out for old canal locks and textile mills. *Main St and Greene Ln*

> **PADDLE OUT** *The Independence Seaport Museum offers four summertime kayak excursions. Admire sky and skyline on a leisurely sunset trip; the 10-mile Petty's Island adventure will test your paddling mettle.*

PENN TREATY PARK

DELAWARE RIVER

PENN'S LANDING

SS UNITED STATES

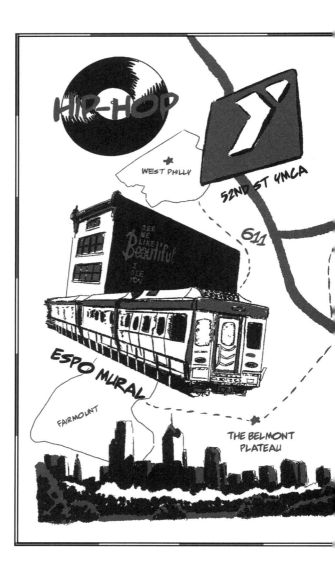

OLD CITY

CHINATOWN

HUNTING PARK

SOUTH STREET

HIP-HOP

Key pieces of the genre's history are written across Philadelphia, where many early icons got their start.

SOUTH STREET

Home for Philadelphia counter-culture since the 1920s. Training ground for the Roots and a generation of stars, including rap-rockers G. Love and Special Sauce and even Kobe Bryant's pre-fame rap group, CHEIZAW. *33rd and Spruce Sts to Front St*

MAX'S STEAKS

As seen in 2015's *Creed* and count-less local rap videos, Max's has long been a hub for real cheese-steaks in North Philly. In 2016, Los Angeles rapper the Game stopped by as a taunt to Meek Mill during their now-infamous rap beef. *3653 Germantown Ave*

THE FIVE SPOT

At the Roots' legendary Black Lily open-mic night, future stars like Jill Scott, Lady Alma and Jazmine Sullivan gave early public performances. The venue burned down in 2007. *5 S Bank St*

SIGMA SOUND STUDIOS

Once the recording home of David Bowie and Philadelphia International, classics from the Roots and Erykah Badu were also recorded here. *212 N 12th St*

PHILADELPHIA MURAL

With references to DJ King Britt and pioneering rapper/radio host Jocko Henderson, the DNA of Philly music culture is embedded in Steve "ESPO" Powers' complex visual rosetta stone. *44 S 2nd St*

BELMONT PLATEAU

In the early days of Philly hip-hop, thumping tunes and wafts of barbecue filled the air at parties on this high grassy hill. Famously referenced in DJ Jazzy Jeff & the Fresh Prince's 1991 hit "Summer-time." *7320 Greenwood Ave N*

52ND STREET YMCA

A West Philly hot spot for hip-hop parties in the '80s. *5120 Chestnut St*

THE GATHERING *Hosted at the historic Rotunda in West Philly on the last Thursday of each month, the city's longest-running hip-hop event showcases the talents of artists, DJs, dancers and graffiti writers across generations. 4014 Walnut St*

PUBLIC ART

The city is chock-full of art: iconic sculptures and historic statues, ambitious mosaics and more than 4,000 murals.

THE THINKER, *Auguste Rodin*
The largest Rodin sculpture collection outside France includes this iconic bronze figure, suspended in eternal contemplation. *Entrance to Rodin Museum*

WE THE YOUTH, *Keith Haring*
Bright figures dance on a white row house. Restored in 2013, it's Haring's only collaborative mural still intact in its original location. *22nd and Ellsworth Sts*

UNTITLED, *Amy Sherald*
This vibrant, six-story depiction of Najee S., a young Black Philadelphian woman, provokes questions about the public gaze. *1108 Sansom St*

MOSAICS, *Isaiah Zagar*
Zagar has been creating dynamic, dreamy mosaic murals since the 1960s. The Magic Gardens hold his life's work, but public works spill into the streets. *South St*

LOVE, *Robert Indiana*
The bold red square of stacked letters has become synonymous with the City of Brotherly Love. *John F. Kennedy Plaza*

CLOTHESPIN, *Claes Oldenburg*
The steel 45-foot-tall everyday object towers elegantly in the shadow of City Hall. *Market St and S 15th St*

A QUEST FOR PARITY, *Branly Cadet*
The 12-foot-tall bronze statue honors Octavius V. Catto, 19th-century civil rights activist and athlete. *City Hall*

FOR PHILADELPHIA, *Jenny Holzer*
EXPLODING PARADIGM
Conrad Shawcross
Words from writers, architects and local students scroll on nine ceiling-mounted screens [Holzer], refracted in the geometric steel sculpture below [Shawcross]. *Comcast Technology Center*

HEAR THE STORIES *The Association for Public Art's Museum Without Walls program features free audio histories of more than 75 sculptures, told by artists, educators, scientists and civic leaders.*
associationforpublicart.org

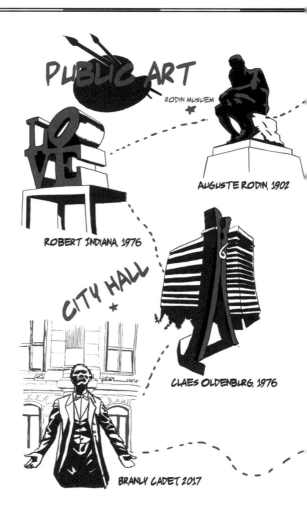

PUBLIC ART

RODIN MUSUEM

AUGUSTE RODIN, 1902

ROBERT INDIANA, 1976

CITY HALL

CLAES OLDENBURG, 1976

BRANLY CADET, 2017

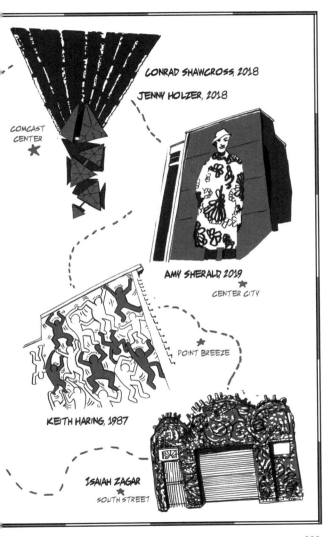

CONRAD SHAWCROSS, 2018

JENNY HOLZER, 2018

COMCAST
CENTER
★

AMY SHERALD, 2019
★
CENTER CITY

POINT BREEZE
★

KEITH HARING, 1987

ISAIAH ZAGAR
★
SOUTH STREET

BENJAMIN FRANKLIN

LOCUSTWALK

BOLT OF
LIGHTNING

BENJAMIN FRANKLIN
BRIDGE

S. BROAD ST

LIBRARY COMPANY
OF PHILADELPHIA

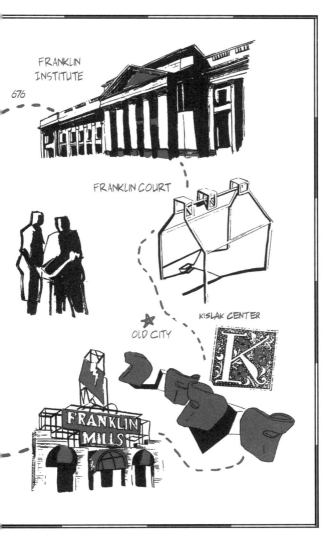

FRANKLIN
INSTITUTE

676

FRANKLIN COURT

KISLAK CENTER

OLD CITY

FRANKLIN
MILLS

BENJAMIN FRANKLIN

Trace the legacy of the writer, printer, political leader, scientist, philosopher, postmaster and Founding Father across the city.

BENJAMIN FRANKLIN (ON A BENCH)

A life-size bronze Ben F. sits reading an issue of *The Pennsylvania Gazette,* which Franklin co-owned and wrote for under aliases. The paper's date: May 16, 1987. Anachronous? Sort of: The statue was first installed in '87. *UPenn campus, 37th St and Locust Walk*

....

LIBRARY COMPANY OF PHILADELPHIA

Began as a "common library" that Franklin and other members of the Junto—predecessor to the American Philosophical Society—assembled. It evolved into the country's first successful lending library. *1314 Locust St*

....

FRANKLIN COURT

A steel "ghost structure" outlines the site of Franklin's brick home, where he died in 1790. Also on-site: The Benjamin Franklin Museum explores his life, plus a reproduction of an 18th-century printing office. *322 Market St*

FRANKLIN INSTITUTE

The science museum includes Franklin's contributions to the subject, such as his electrostatic generator and glass armonica. The Benjamin Franklin National Memorial, featuring a 20-foot-tall marble Franklin, is located in the rotunda. *222 N 20th St*

....

BOLT OF LIGHTNING

Isamu Noguchi's memorial to Franklin arrestingly captures, in 58 tons of stainless steel, the aha moment when Franklin flew a kite with a key attached mid–electrical storm. *N 6th St, base of Benjamin Franklin Bridge*

....

PHILADELPHIA MILLS

Lightning bolt–shaped mall formerly known as Franklin Mills. Legendary graphic designer Milton Glaser went all out; a kite-and-key logo topped the entrances until the last one was dismantled in 2016. *1455 Franklin Mills Cir*

KISLAK CENTER *Browse a collection of Franklin's documents and examples of his printing work, including copies of* Poor Richard's Almanack, *the yearly pamphlet he sold under a pseudonym. The library also displays his mahogany writing desk. Van Pelt-Dietrich Library Center, UPenn*

SPORTS

Today's games are concentrated at the Philadelphia Sports Complex, but the city's rich sports history is all over the map.

FRANKLIN FIELD
Home to the Eagles from 1958 to 1970, the country's oldest two-tiered stadium is still in use, hosting the Penn Relays track and field competition and other events. *233 S 33rd St*

JOE FRAZIER'S GYM
The gym where one of history's greatest fighters perfected his craft. After Frazier retired, he lived above the facility, where the next generation of fighters trained. *2917 N Broad St*

JEFFERSON STREET BALLPARK
The first Major League Baseball game took place here in 1876, despite trees, an embankment on third base and cameos from local animals. *1401-1499 N 27th St*

THE PALESTRA
This 1927 cathedral of college basketball has a rich history of Big 5 contests and other monumental matchups. *235 S 33rd St*

BOATHOUSE ROW
Handsome boathouses line the Schuylkill River's banks. Early morning rowers glide through the water, eyes on the Schuylkill Navy Regatta prize. *1 Boathouse Row*

MCGILLIN'S OLDE ALE HOUSE
Open since 1860, touted as the city's oldest continuously operating tavern. On game days, the two-floor ale house fills with fans. *1310 Drury St*

16TH AND SUSQUEHANNA PARK
This North Philly court spawned street ball legends like Aaron "AO" Owens, Rodney "Hot Rod" Odrick and Bryant "Sad Eye" Watson. *1510 W Susquehanna Ave*

44TH AND PARKSIDE BALLPARK
The field where the Philadelphia Stars played from 1936 to 1952. Hosted Negro League legends Josh Gibson, "Cool Papa" Bell and "Satchel" Paige. *Belmont and Parkside Aves*

ROCKY STATUE *Presented to the city of Philadelphia by Sylvester Stallone in 1982—the same year both he and it appeared in* Rocky III—*the statue now resides next to the Philadelphia Museum of Art.*

SPORTS

FRANKLIN FIELD

JOE FRAZIER BOXING GYM

NORTH PHILLY

JEFFERSON ST
BALLPARK

BREWERYTO

THE PALESTRA

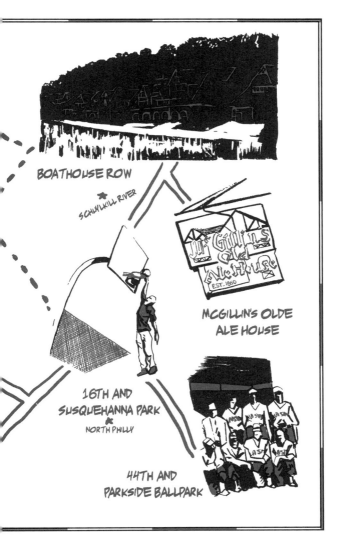

BOATHOUSE ROW

★
SCHUYLKILL RIVER

McGILLIN'S OLDE
ALE HOUSE

16TH AND
SUSQUEHANNA PARK
★
NORTH PHILLY

44TH AND
PARKSIDE BALLPARK

INCLUDING

072 *Neal Santos*

074 *Samantha Hemcher*

075 *Losang Samten*

076 *Raymond Gant*

078 *Ursula Rucker*

081 *Homer Jackson*

082 *Michael Solomonov*

083 *Christopher R. Rogers*

084 *Marangeli Mejia-Rabell*

086 *Bryan Kravitz*

087 *William Peranteau*

089 *Carol Spacht*

090 *Eliot Gilkeson*

092 *Karyn Olivier*

INTERVIEWS

———

*Fourteen conversations with locals of note about jazz,
second chances, urban farming, monuments, Black educators,
woodworking, flagmaking and more*

NEAL SANTOS

RESTAURANT OWNER, PHOTOGRAPHER

I GREW UP in Jersey City but consider Philly my home now. Moved here for school; I've probably spent half my life here.

MY HUSBAND AND I started Farm 51, in Southwest Philadelphia, in 2008. We grow vegetables, flowers. We have about 10 chickens, and we've had a weekly farmstand.

THE FARM DEEPENED my appreciation for food, for photography—and for the city and how to be a neighbor.

THERE'S A LONG history of gardening in the city, which ties into the history of this being a very fertile land back in the day.

THE RESTAURANT industry—and beyond that, this cultural landscape—is so rooted in food and the land itself.

I THINK ABOUT the Lenape, the people who owned this land before our Founding Fathers came, and what kind of things they grew.

MY RESTAURANT, LALO: We're a Filipino food spot, small and mighty.

WE'RE IN THE Bourse in Old City, a historic building right across from the Liberty Bell.

WE DO FAST-CASUAL Filipino food. Rice bowls. There are touches of the seasonality of the farm: Peppers we grow end up in our condiments, like a spicy vinegar.

LALO IS AN extension of my identity as a queer Filipino American living in the city.

MURAL ARTS WAS advertising for a free wedding. I'm broke as shit, so I loved the idea.

WE GOT MARRIED on the Market-Frankford Line. Steve "ESPO" Powers, who did the Love Letter murals all along the line, narrated the train ride, and the first openly gay judge, Dan Anders, officiated.

IT WAS ALMOST like eloping, but publicly. No one was invited. But also everyone was invited.

SAMANTHA HEMCHER

WOODWORKER

ALL THE WOOD that we get at Philadelphia Salvage, and all our stone and marble, is from Philly.

WE SALVAGE IT from old homes, old churches, anything that's getting torn down.

YOU GO TO a job site and there's a whole slew of beautiful wood in the dumpster.

IT'S YELLOW PINE, or oak or mahogany. We take it out and we bring it to the shop.

YOU DON'T WANT it to go into a landfill.

WE PUT IT in a kiln, let it dry.

WHEN IT'S READY, we have to de-nail everything. The wood is probably over 400 or 500 years old. It's from old trees.

THEN WE MILL it, join it, biscuit it and glue it up.

THEN WE DO our final touches. We epoxy it. The customer chooses the stain.

IT'S GREAT TO see people leave with something that they're excited about. I've had people cry, give me hugs.

SOMETIMES YOU GET mad at the wood because it's not going your way. Then you have to figure out: How are you going to fix it?

BECAUSE MOST OF the beams aren't straight or flat. If you go to Home Depot, it's straight most of the time. But the wood that we have here, it's curved. It's bowed.

IN THE OLD buildings, the flooring is mostly yellow pine.

IT'S A VERY dense wood, very heavy.

AFTER YOU CUT into it, the knots, the way the grain goes, it's just beautiful.

THE BUILDING WE work out of was from 1883. The bronze statues in Philly that are on horses—they were made here in this workshop.

LOSANG SAMTEN

TIBETAN BUDDHIST MONK

"MANDALA" MEANS "CIRCLE" in Sanskrit, and in Tibetan we call it *dkyil 'khor*.

SEEING A MANDALA can bring a blessing and wisdom to a person, or harmony to a larger community. The design and colors can represent peace, unity. Every color has a meaning.

I'VE DONE MORE than 1,000 mandalas. I started learning in 1969 at the monastery in India.

IN 1988, I was asked to do one in New York. I ended up doing the first sand mandala for public view in the West.

THEN I CAME to Philadelphia. Some of the people here invited me to be their teacher.

THEY ASKED THE Dalai Lama to let me stay. I was his personal attendant at the time.

I'VE BEEN HERE ever since.

I AM A TEACHER at Chenrezig Tibetan Buddhist Center. We have meditation, we talk and we learn from each other.

I'VE TAUGHT ALL over the place, and people ask, "Do you live in Tibet?"

"NO. PHILADELPHIA." Their eyes go wide.

PEOPLE WHO HAVE never even seen Philadelphia think it's some kind of horrible place, I don't know why.

I ENJOY THE city; I enjoy the neighborhood.

I GREW UP in Tibet, and in my town, Buddhism is everything. The teachers and students there, you just bow down to each other.

WORK TOGETHER, eat together, do the dishes together.

I'VE BEEN DOING this for 30 years.

I GO FROM town to town, carrying that colored sand and trying to give people a little smile.

RAYMOND GANT

COMMUNITY ORGANIZER

SATURDAY WAS ALWAYS hot dogs and beans day.

ABOUT 9 A.M., your mom would be like, "You get out there. Scrub that stoop till it shines."

THEN YOU WOULD get your little allowance, and everybody would be off to the movies.

I GREW UP in the '60s in North Philadelphia. When I think back on those times, our city was more at harmony.

FROM '78 to about '87, I became a major drug dealer. It was a way for a poor family to become rich overnight.

I TOOK THAT idea and ran with it, never understanding the damage I was doing to others.

I WOUND UP in prison for 12 years.

WORD ON THE street was I was going to be dead before my 31st birthday. If you get killed being an OG, you become a legendary name.

IT TOOK GOING to prison for me to find out that I didn't want that. I wanted to live.

WHEN YOU'VE TOLD a story long enough, that becomes the truth for you.

WHEN I CAME home in '98, I went through a program called Landmark Education through the End Violence Project.

I FOUND OUT that I had a discernment of always giving. That's what made me want to change my life.

WILLY BOSTOCK TOOK me to my first Eagles game. October 20, 2002. They were playing Tampa Bay. He was a hope-to-die Eagles fan just like I am.

HE SAID, "What would you like to see happen in your community?"

I SAID, "I'd like to help people living in devastated homes, especially single mothers and senior citizens."

THAT'S HOW the Ray of Hope Project was created. We started helping low-income families that couldn't afford the high cost of structural home damage.

....

WE ALSO CREATED jobs where formerly incarcerated people could learn trades: plumbing, roofing, carpentry.

THE NEIGHBORHOODS were devastated with trash and blight. Ain't no sense in fixing up the houses if we're not going to clean the neighborhoods.

....

THE REST IS history.

....

I DON'T LIVE off luck. I live off of blessings. I'm blessed to be alive.

URSULA RUCKER

POET

I'M A CHILD of hip-hop.

POET. MAMA. FOUR sons. Trying to save the world and its wayward people.

GROWING UP IN Mount Airy, the child of a Black father from the South and Italian mama from Italian Market, it's an interesting amalgamation of things.

PEOPLE SHOULD KNOW there's Black folks living on beautiful blocks with grass and flowers.

EVERYBODY WAS SAFE, and there were always block captains and multiple people looking out for each other.

I HAD A pretty cool experience up until teendom, when truth and reality started coming into view and changing the way that I looked at things.

THE MORE I learned, I looked at my ethnicity and the culture and experience of being "mixed-it."

I USED TO sit in front of my little white Emerson turntable and play my favorite records: Teena Marie, Heatwave, the *West Side Story* soundtrack.

MY OLDEST BROTHER, who was murdered when I was 18, was an avant-garde-jazz connoisseur.

I WOULD ALWAYS sneak into his room and listen to his records and we'd talk about them.

MAN, I WISH we could hang out now. He'd be so proud of me.

WHEN I STARTED listening to Prince at 12, it was a real turning point. I studied the lyrics most of all. The courage and I-don't-give-a-fuck-ness.

PRINCE RAISED ME. Prince raised so many people that he never met.

WITH THE WACKY shit that was going on in the fam, I cherished journal writing. It was my therapy and my escape.

IN MY LATE teens and early 20s, I had chronic headaches. It was because I wasn't writing.

WHEN I REALIZED that, the dam broke and I started letting it all out.

WE NEED TO tell our stories because if we don't, they'll tell it for us, and they tell it wrong.

AND THEN COLLEGE. Learning about my Black self. Taking my first African American studies course, my first intro to Black aesthetics class. Whew. Blew my cap back. I was so mad.

MY FIRST MAJOR recording was with King Britt.

I WAS PERFORMING poetry with music by that point, but I didn't know where I was going to go with it.

KING WAS PAYING attention to what I was doing more than I was. That's what visionaries do.

THIS WAS *Supernatural.* It changed my life.

I AM NOW a poet who is pretty known and does not have a book of poems, but I've got five albums, way over a hundred collaborations and recordings.

IN 2000, there was some protests going on. The Republican Convention was happening here.

I HAD A drink with my homie, Clarence Williams III, Pulitzer Prize–winning photojournalist, at Swanky Bubbles.

I'M LIKE, "Yo, I feel a type of way because I haven't been out there with the people."

HE'S LIKE, "Sis. You hold your picket signs with your poems."

I ALMOST FELL off the chair.

THAT NIGHT HE introduced me to dirty martinis and to that truth about myself.

I KNOW I got a special voice, but you have to learn how to love your own voice—the actual audible voice and the voice from inside. That's the one-two combo.

WE ARE SOUND alchemists and specialists. I take this work mad-serious.

THIS IS MY life's work.

IT INCLUDES THE voice. It includes what I'm saying, how I'm saying it and the activism.

ALL OF IT. Do the work.

HOMER JACKSON

PHILADELPHIA JAZZ PROJECT DIRECTOR

GROWING UP, I was drowning in jazz but didn't know it.

BECAUSE OF THE Great Migration, you get all these people from the South mixed in with Black folks who are already up here, as well as Caribbean Black folk, and you've got a brew.

THEY WERE SEGREGATED, so they had to create their own spots to be able to enjoy themselves.

AROUND EVERY CORNER or so, there was a bar. Bars had jukeboxes and usually a pool table. Squished up behind the pool table certain nights of the week, there would be a jazz organ trio.

I WOULD SEE somebody's mom that we knew, with her slippers on, smoking a cigarette, going into the women's side entrance.

NEXT THING YOU know, you'd see that mom coming out, holding her bag of her 40-ounce or six-pack. They'd be doing the Philly Bop out in the street.

THE BEER SMELL and the cold air coming out of the bar, it's etched in my head.

I DIDN'T KNOW that was jazz. I just thought that was some old ladies.

WHEN I'D JUST graduated, I got a WIIT radio show on Friday nights from midnight to 4 a.m. Nobody wanted to be on Friday nights.

I PLAYED A kaleidoscope of great Black music. A Sun Ra, a Cecil Taylor avant-garde piece. An Art Tatum piece, then maybe a Ray Charles joint.

MOST OF US are still living out our prom night with our music.

THIS CITY HAS always produced musicians. One thing I have hoped to do with the Philadelphia Jazz Project is to get us on the global stage.

I THINK WE can compete with just about anybody in the world. Just give us a chance.

MICHAEL SOLOMONOV

CHEF

THE MOST HUMAN thing that you can do is to be there for somebody in whatever capacity you can.

STEVE, my business partner and best friend—I relied on him through the hardest time of my life. He would pick me up every morning at an AA meeting and drive me into work because I couldn't get from point A to point B without scoring.

WE HAD ALREADY opened Zahav at that point. It could have been a disaster.

I WAS BORN in Israel and raised in Squirrel Hill, Pittsburgh. My dad wanted to move to the land of opportunity.

SQUIRREL HILL WAS pretty Jewish. There were parts of my childhood that I just assumed were normal, like my dad had a weird accent and sometimes we'd have weird shit for dinner.

WHEN I WAS 15 or 16, we moved back to Israel.

I GOT A job working at a bakery. Then I got a job cooking. I was like, *All right, I can do this. I can go to culinary school. I enjoy this. It's fun. It's an actual career.*

WITH ZAHAV, I realized we're not stuck in any tradition. We can look at all of Israel and all the different cuisines and synthesize them on one table.

THAT'S WHAT MODERN Israeli cuisine means. It's taking all those things, putting them together and telling a story of time and place.

IT'S COOL: WE'RE doing Israeli food that nobody was really doing at the time, and it happened in Philly.

THERE'S NOTHING LIKE having New Yorkers come to Philly to have dinner.

PHILLY KEEPS YOU really honest. If you have a shitty product, it doesn't matter what your fucking name is.

CHRISTOPHER R. ROGERS

ORGANIZER, EDUCATOR

PAUL LEROY ROBESON was an entertainer and activist, and some people would say the first Black film star.

HE'S KNOWN FOR being a singer who traveled the world, singing folk songs and Negro spirituals. He's also a noted scholar.

MY ROLE AT the Paul Robeson House is to bring programming that speaks to his legacy.

A LOT OF Black woman educators were part of his family: Sarah Mapps Douglass, Gertrude Bustill Mossell. An ancestry of people who fought for Black progress.

ESLANDA GOODE ROBESON, his life partner, was a trailblazer. She helped introduce Paul into the Harlem Renaissance scene.

THE ROBESONS ARE figures in the Black radical international left that arises in the '30s.

IN 1949, PAUL was performing alongside labor activists in Peek-skill, New York. People tried to call it a Communist rally, and police assaulted numerous people.

THERE'S THIS amazing photo— he's onstage, the workers standing next to him. They know there's snipers, so they're basically saying, "We'll take a bullet for this man."

THIS IS WHEN Robeson becomes the central figure of anti-communist repression.

STARTING IN '66, he's in Philadelphia living with his sister, Marian. Vernoca Michael, our executive director, lived on his block.

SHE REMEMBERS HIM reading the newspaper in multiple languages.

THE ROBESON LEGACY is international. So how do you do this work in a way that is grounded and specific to West Philadelphia, but also make connections between Black resistance and labor struggles happening here and around the world?

MARANGELI MEJIA-RABELL

CURATOR, CULTURAL PRODUCER

PUERTO RICO'S AN island but has this hustle and bustle. The pace of life is very much along the lines of what is here in Philly.

I CAME HERE in 1988.

MY DAUGHTER RELOCATED with me. I was about to turn 14 when I had her.

THAT WASN'T REALLY the norm in 1982, but my parents embraced it.

WHEN I CAME here, I felt happy with my life. I understood the contradictions of colonialism and everything that it entailed, for the most part, as a 20-year-old.

ONCE, A CAB driver tried to guess where I was from. He said, "Don't tell me that you're Puerto Rican."

I FELT THIS sense of pride: "OK, you're insulting my people. What is this about?"

HAVING OUR CULTURE questioned really sparked my curiosity.

THAT SENSE OF responsibility kicked in: This is my new home. How do I contribute?

ARTS AND CULTURE provide a bridge to support people through good times and difficult times.

WITH AFROTAINO Productions, we're giving you the sense of home, family, warmth.

YOU COME TO our events for the energy: The music is popping, the food is good, people are having good conversation. We're just giving folks a space.

HOW DO WE engage independent artists? How do we bring the neighborhood artists? How do we celebrate, working with this premise that everybody's a leader?

THAT'S GUIDED MY work with both AfroTaino and the Philadelphia Latino Film Festival.

WE'RE CELEBRATING ALL this gumbo that we have here with all these different influences and doing it in a very Philly way.

BRYAN KRAVITZ

TYPEWRITER REPAIRMAN

I'M THE FOUNDING partner of Philly Typewriter. Here we are at the corner of Passyunk and Dickinson, and people come to us from all over the world.

WE SELL TYPEWRITERS of all different eras. Exotic machines.

WE DO RESTORATIONS, completely overhaul. There's really nobody doing this, going that deep.

IN 1975, I was in San Francisco, working in a direct-mail plant. A customer watched me with all these dials and everything. He said, "You're mechanically inclined." He brought me a brochure from John O'Connell Trade School in San Francisco.

I MET A typewriter mechanic there. He taught me how to repair an IBM Selectric.

THAT'S THAT RED machine there, all 38 pounds of it.

HE GOT ME a job in a shop, and the rest is history. I took care of 500 machines. I opened the cover up and oiled it and greased it and put it back.

IT WAS CALLED preventive maintenance: This equipment will last forever. It's not like products that are made now, where everything's throwaway.

DURING THE DEPRESSION, the only meat you could ever get was hot dogs. My family sold hot dogs on pushcarts on South Street.

MY GRANDMOTHER WAS on one corner, my father was on one corner, my uncle on one corner. All three of them made a living.

LENNY'S HOT DOGS—if I'd taken it over, I would've been the next generation.

PARENTS DON'T ALWAYS get what you're about. So I went off and figured it out myself.

THIS WORK IS not for the faint of heart. It's learning to use your hands, and your body and your brain working together.

WILLIAM PERANTEAU

SURGEON

I GREW UP in South Jersey, right over the Walt Whitman Bridge. My entire extended family essentially lives within a 50-mile radius of Philadelphia.

MY UNCLE BRIAN is a rheumatologist. I remember thinking, *Wow, this guy's got a cool life. I'd like to do something like what he's doing.*

I'M AN ATTENDING surgeon in the division of general thoracic and fetal surgery at Children's Hospital of Philadelphia.

WE TAKE CARE of fetuses that are diagnosed with abnormalities before birth.

THE HARD DAYS, it helps to put things in perspective: 99 percent of the time, even when a patient doesn't do as well as you'd like, the families know that everybody is working as hard as they can.

MOST DAYS ARE filled with happiness and kids having good outcomes. It's fun to work with kids. And they're very resilient.

I COULD NEVER imagine being in the shoes of these families, and I'm in utter amazement of how strong they are. We get thrown off when my son, Henry, draws on a bedsheet.

WITH THE RESEARCH, I can let my mind wander and think about novel approaches. And we have the resources to test them.

CRISPR IS A gene-editing tool. As it gained attention, it became obvious that we should study applying it before birth.

SOME DISEASES cause irreversible pathology during development. So it would be much better if we could treat those diseases before the pathology has begun.

HOW CLOSE ARE we to clinical application? It's at least five to 10 years away. We need to demonstrate that it's safe.

IF MY JOB was to cure mice of diseases, I'd be hitting grand slams all the time. But you gotta start somewhere.

CAROL SPACHT

HISTORIC INTERPRETER

PEOPLE SEE ONE thing about Betsy. They think she made a flag. Oh my, there's so much more.

A WOMAN OF her time, who made hard choices, who was resilient. A flag maker, an upholsterer and widowed three times.

I HAVE BEEN Betsy at the Betsy Ross House since 2004.

WE HAVE THREE interpreters: when she was a widow after her first marriage as Betsy Ross; at middle age with her second husband as Betsy Ashburn; and I portray the senior Betsy, Betsy Claypoole.

AN INTERPRETER STANDS on a tripod of history, theater and tourism.

I TRAIN NEW Betsys. We go through a rigorous training process, an approximately six-week course.

OUR MANUAL IS called "Being Betsy." It has 75 of the most frequently asked questions.

CHILDREN WANT TO know if you have pets or if you have a favorite food. We actually know from family stories that Betsy Ross liked tomatoes.

PEOPLE ASK, "How did your husband die?" That answer varies according to which Betsy you happen to be. As Betsy Claypoole, my response is, "Well, which husband?"

WE HAVE TO learn about the house, the family relations, her Quaker faith. There are 25 questions just about the flag.

WE'VE MADE ALL the furnishings at Betsy Ross House by hand, historically accurately.

BETSY MAKES ITEMS quickly. That's the only way you can do it.

HER STITCHES ARE simple: the running stitch, a backstitch, a combination stitch between them, then a whipping or a hemming.

WE CAN MAKE a flag about 10 feet long in a week of sewing.

ELIOT GILKESON

CLEANING PROFESSIONAL

I WENT TO school for philosophy and realized I did not want to pursue academia. I was in the restaurant industry and felt very unhealthy with that schedule.

THEN I FOUND this Venn diagram split into circles: what you love doing, what you're good at doing, what you can get paid for and what the world needs.

AT THE CENTER is purpose. I was like, "Cleaning?" It had always been a side hustle for me.

I THOUGHT ABOUT how I could get everything I needed and wanted out of life through cleaning.

IF I MAKE my own business, I'm my own boss and I get to define what being a boss looks like.

OR HOPEFULLY—when we turn West Philly Scrub into a worker-owned collective—what a company without a boss is.

I FOUNDED WEST Philly Scrub as a residential cleaning company with a hyperlocal focus on Cedar Park and the surrounding neighborhoods.

I MOVED TO West Philly 10 years ago. I just felt at home here.

THIS AREA HAS a longstanding history of DIY ethic and community engagement.

WHEN I WAS thinking about what kind of business I wanted to build, I knew I wanted a balance of being very professional while building personal relationships.

THERE IS AN app where you can sign up and it just links you to someone who can come clean your house. You don't even have to be there.

THAT FEELS LIKE the exact opposite of what I'm trying to do.

WE'RE IN OUR clients' homes; it can't just be cold and distant. I want there to be warmth and intimacy, people knowing and respecting each other.

WE'RE ALSO PUTTING a face to domestic work in our community. These are people doing very important, very intimate work.

IT FEELS LIKE this area is growing up, or growing into a new stage of adulthood.

EVERYONE'S FIGURING OUT how to be the best versions of themselves together. And to show up for and lift up the most vulnerable and the most marginalized voices in the community.

I CAME OUT as using they/them pronouns after West Philly Scrub was established, and I changed my name just this past year.

THERE WERE A lot of conversations, with most of our clients already getting it. No one was dismissive.

AS SOMEONE WITH privilege— a white person and with access to owning my own business—I see it as extremely important to say explicitly that West Philly Scrub

is a queer-owned business and we are here for our community.

AND TO LET our clients know that we will not tolerate any homophobia or transphobia or racism.

CEDAR PARK HAS a vibrant queer-identifying community.

I WANT NOT only to uplift my queer community, but also get people paying attention to more marginalized voices taking up space, especially in an entrepreneurial world where it's just not the norm.

I WANT TO see more proudly and loudly queer-owned businesses popping up.

ONE OF MY dreams is to organize a Queer Business Alliance.

IMAGINE HOW COOL Philadelphia could look if more queer, trans, gay, lesbian people had access to business capital and resources.

KARYN OLIVIER

ARTIST, EDUCATOR

I THINK ABOUT artworks like propositions. When I make monuments, they may be grand in scale, but they're humble propositions of another way to look at the world.

IN GRAD SCHOOL, I went straight from making cups and vessels to making installations.

IT SEEMS FUNNY to go from a bowl to a room. But they hold the same things in a lot of ways. A vessel is filled with memories. It's real and it's nostalgic.

I STARTED THINKING about the history of objects. What's presumed? What do we not see? What's the historical baggage?

MY PUBLIC ARTWORK is about these layered, simultaneous, conflicting histories and their fragmentary nature.

MONUMENTS are static, looming. Their materiality is so heavy.

MY CARNATION PIECE, *May 12th,* 1985, is the most ephemeral and most subverting of monuments: When you walk into the museum, you're offered a red carnation.

IN MY CHURCH, on Mother's Day you get a red carnation if your mother's alive or a white one if she's passed.

MAY 12, 1985, is the day the police issued the eviction and the arrest warrants to the MOVE members.

THE FOLLOWING DAY, the most tragic thing happened. Police helicopters dropped a bomb on the MOVE compound. The famous orders: "Let the fire burn."

WE DON'T ALWAYS want to be sitting in Black pain. But what would it mean to be in the day before, when there was celebration, maybe ambivalence, maybe trepidation and worry?

NO ARTWORK CAN make change. You hope it can stir things, hope it's enough to see yourself as beautiful or worthy.

INCLUDED

096   **CORNBREAD AND THE BIRTH OF GRAFFITI**
By John Morrison

101   **WE DON'T CARE**
By Sara Nović

107   **THE AVENUE OF FREEDOM**
By Feminista Jones

115   **PHILADELPHIA'S REDEVELOPMENT:
A PROGRESS REPORT**
By Jane Jacobs

STORIES

Essays and selected writing from
noted Philadelphia voices

CORNBREAD AND THE BIRTH OF GRAFFITI

Written by **JOHN MORRISON**

ONE DAY IN MARCH 1971, North Philly–born artist Darryl "Cornbread" McCray was riding the bus when he opened the local paper and found himself reading about his own death. A young man had been killed in West Philly in an alleged drug-related altercation, and the local news wrongly identified Cornbread as the victim. Determined to prove that he was still very much alive, McCray embarked on a dogged campaign, painting his name on every clean surface he could find in the city of Philadelphia. Amid his efforts to resolve this odd case of mistaken identity, he helped initiate a worldwide art movement.

Today, legal murals and the movement known as street art have largely supplanted graffiti as the dominant form of public art adorning the walls of our cities, with nearly 4,000 produced in Philadelphia in the past three decades. And though graffiti art has been marginalized and largely taken out of its original context, the presence and evolution of illegal graffiti art on the street helped pave the way for its more "respectable" counterparts. While New York [rightfully] gets a lot of credit for the popularization of graffiti art, what many don't know is that the birth of the movement can be traced to the city of Philadelphia and one man. A near-mythic figure in Philly, Cornbread continues to create, speak and teach all around the world, but it is the exploits of his past that have made him a legend.

When McCray was born, in 1953, the city was thriving. At the tail end of the postwar economic boom, most workers could find employment and the social safety net established by Roosevelt's New Deal. Neighborhoods and families grew as a result of the national baby boom, and every weekend, enthusiastic sports fans would pack into landmark stadiums like Philadelphia Municipal and the legendary Connie Mack to watch the Phillies play the Giants or the Brooklyn Dodgers. It was against this backdrop that McCray grew up in the Brewerytown section of North Philly.

In 1965, at the age of 12, McCray was sent off to a juvenile corrections facility called the Youth Development Center. When he arrived, McCray found that the facility was packed with young gang members who had ties to a variety of Philadelphia neighborhoods. McCray, who had a flair for the written word in all its forms, used his talents to build friendships with the gangsters. In a stroke of genius that would have a significant impact on his later craft as a graffiti writer, McCray ingratiated himself to them by ghostwriting flowery love letters to their girlfriends back home.

McCray tried to make the best of his time at the YDC, but he longed for freedom and the comforts of home. Raised by his grandparents, he would complain about the flavorless white bread served in the YDC cafeteria, stating that he preferred his grandmother's cornbread. A cook at the YDC named Mr. Swanson mockingly gave McCray the nickname "Cornbread," a moniker that would follow him for life. Cornbread took to writing his new name all over the facility—bathrooms, hallways, the cafeteria—in large, visible letters alongside the tags of gang members.

After he was released from the YDC, a teenage Cornbread took this penchant for writing his name on walls to the streets, spending his formative years tagging all over Philadelphia. At the time, the city was full of pristine trolley cars and buses and the empty brick walls of massive industrial spaces—all just waiting to be written on. But the gang wars were raging throughout the city, and territories were jealously protected.

Luckily for Cornbread, the cozy relationship he had built with various young gang members now came in handy. Writers were not allowed to tag on walls outside their neighborhoods under any circumstances. In fact, you couldn't even walk safely through some areas without potentially running afoul of the gangs. Cornbread, however, had been gifted a "green pass," allowing him to move and write freely throughout the city in a way that no other artist could. He became the first "all city" writer—whose work can be found across neighborhoods—in history.

Then came March 1971, when Cornbread was distraught to discover that he'd been proclaimed dead. He approached journalists with a copy of his graduation photo, in an attempt to prove that he was in fact alive and well. People were stopping him on the street, exclaiming, "Hey, man! I thought you was dead?!" Catalyzed by this mix-up, Cornbread went on an ambitious tear through the city. Tagging on walls and cop cars, trains and SEPTA buses, he traveled from neighborhood to neighborhood, painting the city with his name.

Still determined to clear up any confusion as to his status among the living and gain even more infamy as a writer, a 17-year-old Cornbread devised a stunt that would help him achieve legendary status. "I knew I had to do something amazingly bizarre to let people know I wasn't dead," Cornbread recalled in a 2014 interview with the *Philadelphia Daily News*. So he went to the Philadelphia Zoo, where he watched a zookeeper use a hose to shower an elephant. Then he made his move: "After three days of watching this, I go to the zoo early in the morning, climb over the fence into the elephant's enclosure," he told the *Daily News*. "I take the paint, start shaking. The balls start rattling. He turns around, he looks at me, doesn't pay attention. I paint 'Cornbread lives' right on his side."

Cornbread was arrested that night, but his boldness and relentlessness made him an icon on the streets. His daring antics even impressed the police, who would stop by his cell to get an autograph. Once he was released, Cornbread continued his campaign. The story of how "CORNBREAD" wound up emblazoned on the Jackson 5's private plane at Philadelphia International Airport is the stuff of Philly cultural lore. The story goes that Cornbread blended in among the fans and autograph-seekers who greeted the band when they landed and, when no one was looking, spray-painted his name on the side of the jet.

Over the years, the legend of Cornbread spread, even after McCray gave up illegally writing on walls, with his eyes set on a normal, less dangerous life. Fast-forward to the '80s, when graffiti was a full-blown cultural phenomenon. Young people were literally writing all over the city. Buses, public buildings, the outside of trains, the inside of trains, deep in the subway tunnels, the sides of bridges, wherever they could. In 1984, when McCray was 31 years old, the city of Philadelphia— acting under the authority of Mayor Wilson Goode—established the Philadelphia Anti-Graffiti Network, which focused on removing graffiti and catching and fining people who were caught writing on public property. In addition to these punitive measures, the organization took a more creative approach to the issue, hosting art contests for talented young people and hiring writers to do legal work.

Seeing how his name, fame and life experiences could be used to help the next generation, Cornbread went to work for the Anti-Graffiti Network, counseling and talking to youngsters about the challenges they were facing. After two years of Goode's "war against wall writers," an artist and Anti-Graffiti Network employee named Jane Golden helped establish Philadelphia Mural Arts, a program that would reshape the city's landscape forever. Carrying on the Anti-Graffiti Network's practice of hiring and collaborating with graffiti writers, Mural Arts commissioned young artists to paint murals, thus channeling the graffiti community's creative talents into a legal and politically acceptable medium. In the decades since the start of this initiative, Mural Arts has been a central force in the beautification of public space in Philadelphia. With thousands of murals created by both local and international artists, Philadelphia reigns supreme as the unofficial mural capital of the world.

When young Darryl McCray began his mission back in the '60s, it would've been impossible to predict that his acts of youthful rebellion would turn him into a folk hero or set in motion a string of events that would change the look and feel of our city and the world beyond. What began as an effort to pass the time, impress girls and assert his own sense of identity would go on to inspire countless creatives, birthing the art form of graffiti as we know it and laying the foundations for a lasting cultural revolution.

JOHN MORRISON is a writer, DJ and sample-flipper. His writing has appeared in NPR Music, Bandcamp Daily, JazzTokyo, Grammy.com and more. He is also the host of *Culture Cypher Radio*, a hip-hop show on UPenn's public radio station, WXPN.

WE DON'T CARE

No one likes us, no one likes us, no one likes us, we don't care. We're from Philly, fuckin' Philly, no one likes us, we don't care.

Written by **SARA NOVIĆ** | **I CAN'T REMEMBER** the occasion for which I first heard Philly's unofficial theme song—sung to the tune of "Found a Peanut," most likely by a crowd of drunk Eagles fans—but I do remember thinking it was fucking depressing. Growing up outside the northeast boundary of the city, I was a self-conscious kid whom the popular kids occasionally sniped at but mostly just ignored. I couldn't imagine a scenario in which I would willingly announce to the world that no one liked me, even if I often believed it to be true.

I took refuge in the emo and punk scene at the city's Electric Factory warehouse, where my friends and I shouted for Dashboard Confessional and Alkaline Trio. We skipped school to see the Dalí centennial at the Philadelphia Museum of Art, walked South Street at dusk, gorging ourselves on water ice and dreaming up the tattoos we'd get when we turned 18. Everyone I knew [myself included] was proud of their working-class roots, but in the hands of teenagers, this pride was quickly bastardized into the notion that being a good student was uncool or somehow disloyal. And I was undeniably a nerd, always with my head in a novel, writing secret poetry, bumbling through the school play because I knew that at least the theater kids would talk to me.

Finally, I graduated high school and made a break for it—no more treading water in a stagnant city where the subway still inexplicably ran on tokens. I went to Boston, then New York City. And I stayed away for a long time.

On the surface, there's a lot to dislike about Philadelphia. It's always been filthy, dirtier still after yet another deep cut to the sanitation budget in 2009 eliminated street cleaning. It's dangerous here, with pockets of the city leveled by the opioid crisis, and far more murders per capita than New York City or Los Angeles. It's poor—the poorest large city in the United States, with 25 percent of residents living below the poverty line. A deeply tangled chicken-and-egg mess of political cronyism, failing public schools, the loss of over 300,000 manufacturing jobs in the latter half of the 20th century and the unrelenting crush of systemic racism and mass incarceration are to blame.

In some ways we're a city marooned. Though Philadelphia and New York are less than 100 miles apart, public transportation between the two leaves something to be desired, with the schedules for SEPTA's Philly to Trenton River line and NJ Transit's Northeast Corridor sometimes failing to line up at all. Many surrounding suburbs have crafted zoning ordinances that block the construction of affordable housing units within town limits, cementing a classist and often racist divide between the city and its suburbs. For its part, the state of Pennsylvania has held tight to its foundational Quaker values, namely a laissez-faire approach to government [except where alcohol is involved—then the grip is vise-like]. As a result, economic growth in Pennsylvania is at only half the rate of the rest of the country since the Great Depression, a statistic so stark that it's difficult to argue it's anything less than intentional. But what works for the rural and agrarian parts of the state leaves an urban center like Philadelphia hamstrung.

No surprise, then, that feelings of abandonment and the city's struggle to keep up with its neighboring metropolises have led to some sizable chips on the shoulders of its residents. My husband likes to say that Philadelphia suffers from Little Brotheritis, being so near to New York and Washington, D.C. And Philadelphians certainly do play the class clown for attention, making headlines for pelting Santa Claus with snowballs, throwing pool parties in dumpsters and stealing police horses. Though the city was once the economic and political epicenter of the nation, today only about a quarter of Americans can correctly identify the Philadelphia skyline. And somewhere along the way, it seems Philadelphians decided it was better to be infamous than forgotten.

But I like to think maybe we're just misunderstood. The blue-collar culture that feels gruff to outsiders is really just a no-nonsense approach to communication. More than that, underdoggedness is axiological to this city since its founding. Philadelphia was once the gathering place of radicals plotting to overthrow the British crown, and George Washington turned the tides of the Revolution on the Delaware River just north of the city limits. Later, the Civil War and the Great Migration made the first free city north of the Mason-Dixon a hub for abolitionism and communities of formerly enslaved people. Today, it's a boon for fresh waves of immigrant and refugee populations from Latin America and Southeast Asia who've injected the city with new life. This includes founders of new Philly-based tech and health care startups like GraphWear and Haystack Informatics, and culinary heavyweights in an already food-famous city, including South Philly Barbacoa's chef, Cristina Martinez [featured on *Chef's Table*], and Ange Branca, a James Beard Award semifinalist for her Malaysian fare.

I remember the first time I missed Philadelphia, really missed it for the city itself, beyond a vague homesickness. I was in Manhattan with a new group of friends much worldlier and wealthier than I was. Usually when we went out, a combination of necessity and obstinance meant I wouldn't eat, not wanting to blow what I knew I could stretch into a week's worth of food money back home on a single meal. [As it turned out, I'd absorbed more Philly attitude than I cared to admit at the time.] But I felt a glimmer of hope the night one of them suggested we go down to Little Italy for dinner. I envisioned the bustling Ninth Street of Philadelphia's Italian Market—its fresh produce stalls, butcheries and cheese shops, porchetta sandwiches, pizza windows and pasticcerie. If Philly's Little Italy was undeniably great, how much more amazing would New York City's be? Better yet, something there would be affordable, and I would finally get to eat dinner, or at least fill up on water ice. But when we arrived on Mulberry Street, there was almost nothing there—a few sit-down restaurants and a few strands of red, white and green fairy lights to mark the ghost of what once was.

A slow rate of change can be frustrating for Philly residents, but it also means a melding of old and new unique to this city—in other more rapidly gentrifying places, historical sites and cultural hubs might have been razed to make way for oligarchs' condos. Places like the Italian Market, which dates to the 19th century and remains one of the oldest and largest open-air markets in the U.S. It's not only still bursting with great Italian food but is also home to an influx of other international flavors, including Martinez's tacos and enough Vietnamese food to earn the alternate nickname "Little Saigon." In Manhattan, Little Italy was subsumed by Chinatown. Here, we have the space, affordability and rooted communities to keep the best of both.

I moved back to Philadelphia in 2017, just in time to see the Eagles make their Super Bowl run. Every game, I'd walk over to a high school

friend's house to crowd on the couch and watch. More of a baseball fan myself, I'd never really liked the stop-and-go nature of football, but this city's love for its Eagles is nothing if not contagious. And there was that song again: Whenever they scored a touchdown, someone would head off the Eagles' official fight song, which flowed right into "No One Likes Us."

A version of "No One Likes Us," it turns out, was originally a soccer chant for the English team Millwall, set hilariously to the tune of Rod Stewart's "Sailing." Millwall fans took unruly to another level—in the 1960s, one even threw a grenade onto the pitch. The Philly adaptation of the song also grew out of a soccer fan club, the Sons of Ben [as in Franklin], who formed online before the city even had a soccer franchise and who now cheer on the Philadelphia Union from the river end of Subaru Park.

But the song made a home for itself far beyond soccer, and as the Eagles' success continued through the playoffs that year, it was a staple in the bars and city streets. Then our star quarterback, Carson Wentz, tore his ACL. It was up to second-string Nick Foles, who hadn't played that season, to take on Tom Brady and Bill Belichick's Patriots, one of the winningest teams of all time.

When the Eagles won, the fans flooded the streets and all manner of stupid behavior ensued. The national media tore the city apart, but then again, didn't they always? What looked like chaos from the outside was the most harmonious I'd ever seen the city's residents. A few days later, the team threw an officially sanctioned parade. Our apartment at the time was on the route, and our friends showed up early to claim space on our stoop. I poured coffee for the cops who'd come in asking to use our bathroom. Our upstairs neighbors had painted a bedsheet with the phrase "Big Dick Nick"—the city's nickname for Foles—and hung it out the window. As he passed by on the double-decker bus, Foles laughed and snapped a picture.

The parade ended at the steps of the Philadelphia Museum of Art, where the team's center, Jason Kelce, clad in a Mummers suit and hat, presented a laundry list of negative things people had said about the Eagles and the odds they'd overcome, then led a million-person singalong of "No One Likes Us."

In that moment, Kelce embodied the essence of the city beyond football: His sequined outfit is the traditional celebratory garb of the city's large populations of Ellis Island–era working-class immigrants, his place on the museum's steps a callback to the city's favorite claim to fame: Rocky Balboa. For a moment, Philly was the top dog.

Maybe that's one of the reasons why sports are so beloved here: It's a forum where Little Brotheritis is actually productive. So many iconic American athletes—from Michael Jordan and Michael Phelps to Simone Biles—are younger siblings, learning from, competing with and eventually surpassing their older brothers and sisters.

Sometimes, being the underdog can be powerful. At the very least it makes the game more exciting. For my part, I've learned that Philadelphia, like a cheesesteak wit, can be an acquired taste. But I'm happy to be here, to bring my son up on a block where my mortgage is cheap, the magnolia trees bloom bright pink and the neighbors and I can chat about how big he's grown. And when the day comes that someone out on the playground pokes fun at him, I hope I can teach him not to care.

SARA NOVIĆ is the author of *Girl at War* and *America Is Immigrants*; her second novel, *True Business*, is forthcoming. She has an MFA in fiction and literary translation from Columbia University and lives in South Philly.

THE AVENUE OF FREEDOM

Written by **FEMINISTA JONES**

I FIRST VISITED Belmont Mansion in Northwest Philadelphia for an elegant event celebrating Nigerian Independence Day. Pop-up tents decorated the sprawling grounds, and attendees were decked out in clothing with beautiful African prints. The staff greeted us with warm smiles as we sipped sparkling drinks and dined on fine Nigerian cuisine. Afrobeats played in the background as partygoers exchanged hugs and made introductions.

The hostess had carefully chosen the venue not only for the central location, well-kept grounds and reasonable prices, but also for its significance. That day, I learned that the mansion was once a safe house for people who'd escaped slavery and now the home of the Underground Railroad Museum. I thought I knew most of the city's historical landmarks. But this discovery inspired me to learn more about the places that I walk by every day.

When I decided to move to Philly, I did so with thoughtful consideration of its rich history, its thriving urban culture and its unique soul. Delicious food, a robust underground arts scene and a key role in shaping America into what she is today placed the city high on my list. This isn't the first time I have lived in Philly: I attended the University of Pennsylvania as an undergraduate student at the turn of the millennium. While exploring Philadelphia as a student, I learned more about the city than any textbook had ever taught me—mostly through talking with residents and community members whose families had been there for generations. Connecting with students and community leaders in some of the poorest areas of the city affirmed my decision to pursue social work as a career, but I didn't plan to stay. Though it took nearly 15 years, I came back to the city knowing I would be welcomed to make a new home for me and my son.

Philadelphia's cultural diversity was a huge draw for me. Black residents make up 43.6 percent of the population, more than in any other large American city. One cannot ignore how deeply Black culture is embedded into the city's vibe, visible in its music, art and food. Even the local dialect: "Jawn"—the popular, uniquely Philly word that can mean a person, place or thing—comes directly from the African American Vernacular English used by Black Philadelphians. The famous "Philly beard"? Inspired by Black Muslim men wearing traditional facial hair. When people want a Philadelphia cheesesteak and ask if they should go to Pat's or Geno's, Philly natives are quick to redirect them to places like Black-owned Max's Steaks on Broad and Erie. And if you venture into the Free Library, the Philadelphia Museum of Art or the Land Title Building on 14th and Chestnut, you may not realize those buildings were designed by Julian Francis Abele, the first Black man to graduate with a B.A. in architecture from UPenn.

WHY AREN'T THE STORIES OF BLACK PEOPLE FIGHTING FOR LIBERATION HERE A BIGGER PART OF THE HISTORY TAUGHT IN SCHOOLS? WHY AREN'T THESE STORIES CELEBRATED AND TOLD?

Unfortunately, the city has also struggled with poverty for generations and has the highest poverty rate of large cities: 26 percent of residents live at or below the poverty line. I moved back here to do what I could to help as a social worker, focusing on poverty, homelessness and hunger. I recognized the desperate needs of hundreds of thousands of people eager to improve their lives. It's hard to ignore the disparities when walking or driving around the city: The food deserts, the profusion of abandoned houses and the asbestos-ridden school buildings are all tied to classism, racism and systematic neglect.

As I had done as a student, I began to spend more time talking to Black people who were born and raised here and came from generations who struggled through economic disenfranchisement. Their stories resonated with me as someone who was also born into poverty, deepening my motivation. My work has included educating people about the city's history with the hope that they find inspiration in the stories of people who helped shape our city. When people walk down Cecil B. Moore Avenue or the "Avenue of Freedom" [6th Street and Market], they may not fully appreciate the history behind the naming of these streets. I want to change that.

While known for the Liberty Bell, Benjamin Franklin and other colonial Americana, Philadelphia is also a city built on stories of freedom fighting and triumph. After my visit to Belmont Mansion, I wanted to learn more about Philadelphia as an epicenter of protest, resistance and liberation, particularly for Black Americans. What started as online research soon led me to talks at bookstores like Uncle Bobbie's Coffee and Books and the Free Library as well as lectures and panels at the University of Pennsylvania and the Kimmel Center. When it comes to historical narratives of the Black experience in the United States, I'm a bit of a nerd, so I keep these weeknight events on my radar. The fact that there are so many is one of my favorite things about Philly.

I've long known that as early as 1639, enslaved Africans worked and made significant contributions to the development of the city. By the Revolutionary War, enslaved and freed people made up 8 percent of the population. As their numbers grew, as a result of migration of African refugees from Haiti and southern Colonies, Philadelphia's government enacted racist Black Codes and restrictive gradual manumission laws that limited mobility and achievement for Black people. Even in this northern city where the Declaration of Independence was signed, liberty was reserved for those deemed worthy of it.

But these limitations didn't stop Black Philadelphians from fighting to make the world better for all people. Theirs was a city that their kinfolk to the south dreamed of: a place to escape to and start new lives as free people. Many of those who had been able to integrate into society as free people helped others find homes, employment and social connections that would allow them to survive and even thrive. The Free African Society, for example, was founded by Richard Allen, a man born into slavery who eventually purchased his freedom. Along with Absalom Jones, Allen formed the religious society with the goal of helping newly freed Africans and their descendants get situated and established in the city. They provided care for orphans, tended to the sick and elderly, supported widows and developed educational and training programs for younger people looking to learn trades and start their own businesses. The first of its kind in Philadelphia, the Free African Society was one of the earliest examples of a Black-operated mutual aid organization in America.

As the society moved toward more Quaker values, Allen, a Methodist, left the group and went on to establish the African Methodist Episcopal Church at Bethel AME on Sixth Street. Now known as Mother Bethel AME, the church became a fixture in the historic Seventh Ward, a neighborhood W.E.B. Du Bois famously studied and wrote about in *The Philadelphia Negro*. I grew up in church, and though I no longer identify as Christian, I still appreciate and honor the importance of the "Black Church" to not only the faith communities it serves, but also the larger historical fights for civil rights and freedom. Known for its stained-glass windows and antique pews, Mother Bethel feels like a classic novel's depiction of an old church—with the priceless acoustics, a whisper becomes a shout, and you may find yourself transported to a 19th-century Bible study that served as cover for a secret meeting about a new group of refugees coming into the city.

Considering that Christian faith was a guiding force for the majority of enslaved people and the church was a central institution—for community development, resistance planning and organizing in addition to religious practice—for Allen and Jones to become ordained at a time of turmoil in the Colonies was no small feat. The society would go on to inspire and support abolition efforts and strengthen the work of abolitionists from Philadelphia and all over the ever-growing country. The society had strong support from white Philadelphian abolitionists as well, which helped them expand their reach and the scope of their work.

Abolition in Philadelphia was crucial to the power and success of the larger abolitionist movement. The Philadelphia Female Anti-Slavery Society, which formed in 1833, was one of only a few racially integrated abolitionist societies in the country. Though mostly white, the society welcomed several middle-class and wealthy free Black women who shaped the organization's more radical approach to abolition. The society was also known for financially supporting

local schools for Black girls, and, like the Free African Society, it provided mutual aid to enslaved Black people who had escaped to the city. As the society began to do more grassroots work, a rift formed between the white and Black women, and the most notable member, suffragist and abolitionist Lucretia Mott, was among those who didn't think aiding Southern refugees was the society's purpose. Mott, who has a street named for her in Cheltenham, was an early women's rights and voting rights activist and a Quaker abolitionist. Still, the society has been cited as an early influence on American feminism, and the contributions of the Black female leadership is worth noting, as Black women are too often erased from feminism's origin stories.

If it were not for societies like these, Ona Judge would not likely have been able to escape from George Washington's plantation and survive. I first learned this story at a talk hosted by the Africana studies department at UPenn with Erica Dunbar, who wrote about Judge in the book *Never Caught*. Washington is often portrayed as an enslaver by marriage, as if this makes him less complicit in slavery. To learn that he was seemingly obsessed with finding Judge and bringing her back to his home troubled me: What was it about her, or at least his connection to her, that motivated him to expend so much energy attempting to capture her? Washington devoted several years and considerable funds to retrieving Judge but never caught her. As secretive as this effort was, Washington was willing to risk his reputation and compromise his political standing to bring her back. Judge relied on the abolitionists in Philadelphia and New Hampshire to evade the people sent to capture her.

Philadelphian abolitionists set up intricate networks of safe houses, including Belmont Mansion, to help people like Judge. Belmont Mansion was built by William Peters. His son, Richard, a member of the Pennsylvania Society for the Abolition of Slavery, purchased enslaved people in order to free them and hid refugees in the mansion's attic. Were it not for the efforts of abolitionists, Black Philadelphians would have endured the horrors of enslavement for much longer than they did, and the state's laws might not have changed until emancipation was federally mandated in 1863.

During the civil rights movement, freedom fighting in Philadelphia continued and played a critical role in labor rights activism. Martin Luther King Jr. was introduced to Mahatma Gandhi's Satyagraha, an approach that centers nonviolence in activism, at Philadelphia's Fellowship House [now known as Fellowship Farm]. Meanwhile, Cecil B. Moore, the president of Philadelphia's NAACP chapter from 1963 to 1967, cut his teeth as a Temple University-educated lawyer who advocated primarily for poor Black people living in North Philadelphia. A military man, he was known for pushing back against the "nonviolent" narrative and calling for more-aggressive actions to secure equality for Black Philadelphians. The university later named its main thoroughfare after him.

Moore notably welcomed Malcolm X at a time when Philly was a prominent city for the Nation of Islam, with a dozen affiliated mosques. When the leader, Elijah Muhammad, died, his son W. Deen Mohammed broke away from the NOI and brought many members to a more traditional, orthodox practice of Islam. He founded Masjidullah, one of the largest Black mosques in the nation, here in Philadelphia. Today, it serves not only as a house of worship, but a community center for Black Philadelphians in need of help. Philadelphia has the highest concentration of Black Muslims in America, and their influence on the city's culture and progress is vast. Black Muslims in Philly are members of local activist groups like Black Lives Matter and the Black and Brown Workers Cooperative and have engaged in mutual aid projects that have helped many Philadelphians living in poverty.

THERE IS NO PHILADELPHIA AS WE KNOW IT WITHOUT BLACK PHILADELPHIANS, AND THOSE OF US WHO LIVE AND WORK HERE OWE IT TO THOSE WHO RISKED EVERYTHING IN THE NAME OF FREEDOM TO NEVER FORGET THEM.

After hundreds of years, Black Philadelphians still face strong obstacles in their pursuit of happiness. Many still encounter the remnants of racist practices that have disenfranchised them and left them to live in the margins, scarcely scraping by. Many of their historical neighborhoods—like Center City, Graduate Hospital,

Point Breeze and Powelton Village—have been gentrified, and Black Philadelphians have been pushed out.

There are times when I am walking around Old City or Queen Village and can't help but think of the generations of Black Philadelphians whose labor designed and built the cityscape as we know it today, but who never received fair compensation or credit. It's difficult to walk along Front Street, particularly the intersection of Front and Market streets, where enslaved Africans were auctioned to local wealthy buyers. Heading down to Penn's Landing one day, I was caught off guard when I saw a historical marker that described the London Coffee House: "Scene of political and commercial activity in the colonial period, the London Coffee House … served as a place to inspect Black slaves recently arrived from Africa and to bid for their purchase at public auction." Other people just walked past, not even noticing the marker or the history it invoked.

I don't believe enough is taught about the history of Black people fighting against racism and for liberation here in Philadelphia. In 2018, I visited a school and asked the class if they knew who Cecil B. Moore was. None of the students could answer, yet they were all familiar with the street named for him. Why aren't the stories of Black people fighting for liberation here a bigger part of the history taught in schools? Why aren't these stories celebrated and told? I envision a mobile classroom that could visit not only schools, but houses of worship, bookstores, even Fairmount Park so more people could learn about Allen, Moore and others.

Galvanized by police brutality, racial discrimination in housing and education, mass incarceration and other civil rights violations, Black Philadelphians continue to carry on a tradition of resistance deeply rooted in the city's legacy of freedom fighting and organizing. The fire that burned in the souls of those who resisted racial oppression in the 18th century flames on in the spirits of today's youth. When I went to a rally at Love Park, I encountered the Philadelphia Student Union, a collective of young people advocating for high-quality education and better conditions in the city's schools. Seeing this work continue with the next generation of activists gives me great hope for the future.

Living in Philadelphia has enriched my life in ways I had not predicted. I rest better, breathe easier and actually talk to my neighbors on a regular basis. I've gotten to know groups of Black Philadelphians who love to travel, garden, experience the arts and focus on living healthier lives. There is no Philadelphia as we know it without Black Philadelphians, and those of us who live and work here owe it to those who risked everything in the name of freedom to never forget them. As the new generation of freedom fighters surely understands, it costs nothing to pay homage to those who came before us and keep their legacy alive.

FEMINISTA JONES is a Philadelphia-based author, activist and Ph.D. student at Temple University in the Africology and African American studies department.

PHILADELPHIA'S REDEVELOPMENT: A PROGRESS REPORT

Written by **JANE JACOBS**

ONCE UPON A TIME the general problem of the City Chaotic looked so simple.

Boulevards and civic monuments were going to create the City Beautiful. After that proved insufficient, regional plans were to create the City Sensible. These proved unadoptable and now we are struggling, sometimes it seems at the expense of everything else, to improvise the City Traversible.

And still the deserts of the city have grown, and still they are growing, the awful endless blocks, the endless miles of drabness and chaos. A good way to see the problem of the city is to take a bus or streetcar ride, a long ride, through a city you do not know. For in this objective frame of mind, you may stop thinking about the ugliness long enough to think of the work that went into this mess. As a sheer manifestation of energy it is awesome. It says as much about the power and doggedness of life as the leaves of the forest say in spring. Hundreds of thousands of people with hundreds of thousands of plans and purposes built the city and only they will rebuild the city. All else can only be oases in the desert.

Philadelphia is a city, perhaps the only U.S. city thus far, that has looked at this appalling fact and begun to deal with it.

In Philadelphia, a redevelopment area is not a tract slated only—or necessarily primarily—for spectacular replacements. In short, it is not simply to be an oasis. Most certified areas include a great deal of acreage that never will have a magic wand waved suddenly over it. Some of Philadelphia's redevelopment money is to be spent thinly and very, very shrewdly in interstices of these areas to bring out the good that already exists there or play up potentialities.

The Philadelphia approach also means a busybody concern with what private developers will be up to next: a jump ahead. To keep the desert from spreading interminably, plans and persuasion for thinly settled outer reaches have already been marshaled. Downtown, Penn Center is an example of this approach. By the time the Pennsy decided to remove its tracks and old Broad St. Station, the planning commission was ready with a suggested scheme and through thick and thin it has never let the essentials of the scheme get lost. It has not been easy, but the gain to the city—and the developers—is incalculable.

Whether a new oasis is public or private, Philadelphia's planners look at it not simply as an improvement, but as a catalyst.

Little good can happen to people or to buildings when a sense of neighborhood is missing. Philadelphia's inexpensive devices toward the enormous gain of restoring the neighborhood to the desert may be its greatest contribution to city planning. As part of this aim, the city's public housers are not rearing alien institutions unrelated to the surrounding murk, nor are they using public housing as social and economic wall-building to dam off portions of the city. Instead, the projects are being sunk into their neighborhoods, to help rehabilitate, not eviscerate, them.

In this atmosphere of hope for the city, the initiative of private citizens seems to be thriving in the little and in the large. The new food distribution center will not only be a huge improvement in its own right and serve as a two-way catalyst [removing blight from several parts of the city, instituting improvement in another], but it is an unprecedented display of public-spirited, private rebuilding.

What is happening in Philadelphia is of such scope and involves so many people there is no neat and easy explanation for what started it or why. Physical rejuvenation of the city seems to be related to a booming hinterland, dissatisfaction with long do-nothing, a surge of municipal reform and citizen activity, the jolt of the war years.

There is something else you cannot help seeing as you walk about the city or listen to its planners, its architects and its businessmen. Philadelphia's abrupt embrace of the new, after long years of apathy, has by some miracle not meant the usual rejection of whatever is old. When a city can carry on a love affair with its old and its new at once, it has terrific vitality.

Here is Philadelphia Architect Louis I. Kahn, talking about order within the city:

"The order of our city must be the ordering of movement. *But movement implies stopping—the objective of movement.* The major idea of the center of the city should be places for stopping. Clearings are readable places, orienting places; around them real estate thrives.

"There are *degrees* of movement too in a city—continuous and staccato. But today zoning does not take in the most important third of the land: the streets. Design of the street is no further advanced than in the day of the horse.

"The street is an architectural problem, as well as a planning problem. With appropriations for streets must come garages which are extensions of the street, part of the street. They are the docks of the traffic rivers. Design of the street and its docks, ramps and levels, distinctions among flowing, staccato and stopping streets would give rise to an architecture of movement just as expressive as Carcassonne's architecture of defense. Within that order buildings could take on any form without destroying the order and readability of the city."

Philadelphia is a long way from becoming Kahn's city of movement, but the seeds of this thinking are germinating.

Here is Harry A. Batten, chairman of the board of N.W. Ayer & Son, and a leader in the food distribution center project, talking about the high-powered Greater Philadelphia Movement:

"Benjamin Franklin was a printer who became a diplomat and Alexander Hamilton a bookkeeper who became a statesman. Men of practical affairs who learned how to make their abilities effective on a higher stage had a lot to do with building this country. A good deal of it happened right here in Philadelphia.

"One of the biggest jobs right now for men who have this drive is the job of rebuilding our cities, and that idea has caught hold in Philadelphia. It has nothing to do with the usual city boosting. These are not a bunch of narrow fellows putting on pep talks or out to make a quick buck or protect the status quo. They are educated men who care deeply about the city. For instance, I would say our brilliant crop of younger bankers is giving outstanding leadership. They have everything you don't expect a banker to have unless you are a daughter of a banker."

Here is Executive Director Edmund Bacon of the city planning commission, talking about the impetus to planning:

"The first efforts for revitalized planning in Philadelphia came not from the government, but from a small group of young citizens. Finally a group of about 60 organizations petitioned the city council to establish a planning program. From the first moment the commission sat in formal session it was aware that it occupied its place because of the work of citizens' groups. The organizations which worked on the ordinance became a formal Citizens' Council on City Planning, which has since grown to 200 civic organization members. The interaction of this group and independent citizens' groups, supporting or criticizing, have given much of the strength to the planning program.

"The efficiency and order which the planner desires is less important than the preservation of individual democratic liberties and, where the two are in conflict, the demands of the democratic process must prevail."

JANE JACOBS was an urbanist, activist and writer. She is best known for the groundbreaking ideas in her 1961 treatise, *The Death and Life of Great American Cities.* This story originally appeared in *Architectural Forum*'s July 1955 issue.

INDEX

INDEX

16th and Susquehannah Park 67

44th and Parkside Ballpark 67

48th Street Grille 10

52nd Street YMCA 60

76ers 38

A Novel Idea 8

Abele, Julian 31, 108

Abolitionism 27

Abyssinia 15

Allen, Richard 109

Amalgam Comics & Coffeehouse 16

Anderson, Marian 42

Angelo's Pizzeria 28

Apiary 6

Apple Butter Frolic 6

Architecture 5, 31

Ars Nova Workshop 18

Art in the Age 17

Ba Le Bakery 28

Bacon, Edmund 40, 117

Bardo Pond 7, 17

Barnes Foundation 7, 18, 31

Bartram's Garden 55

Baseball 38, 67

Basketball 38, 48, 67

Belmont Mansion 107, 113

Belmont Plateau 60

Benjamin Franklin Parkway 37

Benner, Conrad 21

Bertino, Marie-Helene 6

Betsy Ross House 89

Big Blue Marble 8

Bissinger, Buzz 6

BlackStar Film Festival 6

Blue Cross River Rink 19

Blue Stoop 21

Boathouse Row 10, 67

Bob & Barbara's 15

Boyds 10, 15

Boyz II Men 7

Brewery ARS 10

Brewerytown Beats 16

Breyers 26

Brownlee, David B. 37

Bucket of Teeth 45

Busch, Birdie 7

Cadet, Branly 61

Cafetería y Panadería Las Rosas 15

Cake Life Bake Shop 10

Campo's Deli 28

Cheesesteak 28, 33

CHEIZAW 60

Cira Center 31

Citywide Special 9, 15

Clark Park Farmers' Market 18

Clay Studio 19

Cole, Harriet 45

Colored Girls Museum 18

Corruption 40

Couch Tomato 10

Crown and Feather Tattoo 21

Cuttalossa 17

Dalessandro's 14

Damo Pasta Lab 54

Deacon, The 8

Delaware River 55

Di Bruno Bros. 33

Dilworth, Richardson 34

Dirty Frank's 19

DJ Bran 21

DJ Jazzy Jeff & the Fresh Prince 60

Dock Street West 15

Du Bois, W.E.B. 36, 110

Eagles 9, 29, 38, 46, 67, 101, 105

Eastern State Penitentiary 6

Elixir Coffee 8

Erving, Dr. Julius 48

Esherick House 31

EverybodyFights 8

Fairmount Park 6

Fante's Kitchen Shop 16

Farber, Paul M. 20

Feminista Jones 107

Feria del Bario 6

Fiore Fine Foods 54

Fisher Fine Arts

Library 31
Fitler Club 8
Five Spot 60
Flyers 5, 38
Foles, Nick 105
Fork 10
Four Seasons 8
Frankfort Yellow
    Jackets 29
Franklin Court 66
Franklin Field 67
Franklin Fountain 10
Franklin Institute 66
Franklin, Benjamin
    24, 27, 66
Frazier, Joe 38, 67
Free African
    Society 109
Friday Saturday
    Sunday 7, 10
Furniture making 27
G. Love and Special
    Sauce 60
Gant, Raymond 76
Gathering, The 60
Geno's Steaks 9, 33, 108
Germantown
    Friends 27
Gilkeson, Eliot 90
Goldie 7, 28
Grip the Raven 45
Gritty 5, 7
Gross, Terry 20, 35
Hall & Oates 7
Hardena 10
Haring, Keith 61
Harley, Rufus 7
Harriet's Bookshop 8
Hemcher,
    Samantha 74

High Street on
    Market 7, 28
Hip-hop 21, 60, 78
Ho, Wai-Jee 21
Holzer, Jenny 61
Honeysuckle 21
Humphry's Flag
    Company 16
Indego 6
Independence Hall
    5, 6, 20, 25, 27, 40
Independence
    Seaport
    Museum 55
Indiana, Robert 61
Isgro Pastries 14, 33
Italian food 54
Italian Market 33,
    78, 103
Iverson, Allen 38
Jackson, Homer 81
Jacobs, Jane 115
Jazz 19, 48, 81
Jefferson Street
    Ballpark 67
Jezabel's Cafe 10
Jinxed 16
John Heinz National
    Wildlife Refuge 19
John's Roast Pork
    14, 28
John's Water Ice 14
Johnny Brenda's 19
Josesph Fox
    Bookshop 8
Joshua, Tommy 21
Judge, Ona 110
Junto 24
Kahn, Louis 31, 116
Kalaya 14, 33

Kelce, Jason 105
King Britt 7, 60, 79
Kraiza, Robert 21
Kravitz, Bryan 86
La Colombe 8
LaBan, Craig 20
Laurel 15
Le Bus Bakery 10
Le Virtu 54
Leather Apron
    Club 24
Lenape tribe 46, 55
Levine, Judith 9
Liberty Bell 10, 25,
    72, 109
Library Company of
    Philadelphia 66
Lokal 8
Lyons, John 21
M. Finkel &
    Daughter 17
Magic Gardens 7, 61
Maillardet's
    Automaton 45
Malenka, Sally 20
Manayunk Towpath 55
Manufacturing 26
Marsh + Mane 16
Martha 15
Martha Graham
    Cracker Cabaret 19
Massiah, Louis 20
Max's Steaks 60, 108
Mayson, Trapeta
    B. 20
Mazarin 7
McCray, Darryl
    "Cornbread" 96
McGillen's Olde Ale
    House 67

Mejia-Rabell, Marangeli 84
Menagerie Coffee 8
Mezzacappa, Dale 9
Middle Child 15, 28
Mill, Meek 7, 20, 60
Mina's World 10
Minima 17
Mitchell & Ness 17
Mohammed, W. Deen 111
Monument Lab 20
Moon + Arrow 17
Moore, Cecil B. 109, 112
Morrison, John 96
Mother Bethel AME Church 110
Mott, Lucretia 110
MOVE 35, 49
Mr. Joe's Cafe 28
Mr. Martino's Trattoria 54
Muhammed, Elijah 111
Mummers Parade 6, 44
Mural Arts 45, 100
Museum Without Walls 61
Mütter Museum 19, 45
Nabisco 26
Niederkorn Antique Silver 17
Nifty Fifty's 10
North Philly Peace Park 21
Nović, Sara 101
Nuevofest 6

Odunde 18
Old Baldy 45
Oldenburg, Claes 61
Olivier, Karyn 92
Omoi Zakka 17
Oscar's Tavern 14
Osteria 54
OutFest 6
Ox Coffee 8
P's and Q's 7
Palestra 67
Palizzi Social Club 54
Parc 15
Parking 34
Pat's King of Steaks 9, 28, 33
Pendergrass, Teddy 7
Penn Relays 67
Penn Treaty Park 55
Penn, William 32, 55
Penn's Landing 55
Pennsylvania Packet 47
People's Paper Co-op 21
People's Philadelphia Cookbook 41
Peranteau, William 87
PFS Roxy Theater 18
Philadelphia Experiment, The 7
Philadelphia Flower Show 6
Philadelphia magazine 6
Philadelphia Mills 66
Philadelphia Museum of Art 6, 20, 31, 101, 105

Philadelphia Salvage 74
Philadelphia Stars 67
Philadelphia Zoo 98
Phillies 38
Philly Craft Beer Festival 6
Pho 75 15
Picanha Brazilian Steakhouse 10
Pitchers Pub 10
Pizzeria Beddia 14, 28
Pod Philly 8
Poor Richard's Almanack 66
Powers, Steve "ESPO" 60
Pretzels 6
PSFS Building 31
Public art 6, 20, 61, 92, 96
Quakers 27, 89, 103, 110
RAIR 21
Reading Terminal Market 15
Ready to Ride 19
ReAnimator 8
Res Ipsa Cafe 54
Retrospect Vintage 17
Rich, John 20
Rittenhouse Spa & Club 8
Ritual Shoppe 17
Rizzo, Frank 33, 35
Rocky 33, 44, 67
Rocky 50k Fat Ass Run 19
Rodin, Auguste 61

Rogers, Christopher R. 83
Roney, Jessica 21
Roots Picnic 6
Roots, The 7, 60
Ross, Betsy 89
Row house games 36
Row houses 5
Rowland Company 16
Rucker, Ursula 76
Sabbatical Beauty 17
Sabrina's Café 10
Sam's Morning Glory Diner 15
Samten, Loseng 75
San Miguel, Carmen Febo 20
Sanchez, Sonia 49
Sandwiches 15, 28, 41
Santa 46
Santos, Neal 72
Sarcone's 28
Savery, William 27
Schuylkill Navy Regatta 67
Schuylkill River 6, 7, 21, 55
Schuylkill River Trail 7, 55
Scott, Jill 7, 60
Scribe Video Center 20
Scullion, Sister Mary 9
SEPTA 6, 98, 102
Shawcross, Conrad 61
Sherald, Amy 61
Shish-Kabob Palace 10
Sielski, Mike 21

Sigma Sound Studios 60
Slang 39
Slavery 27
Soap Lady 45
Solomonov, Michael 82
South Philly Barbacoa 10, 33, 103
South Street 60
Spiral Q 19
Sporting heartbreak 32, 38
Spracht, Carol 89
Spruce Street Harbor Park 10
SS *United States* 55
St. Oner's 10
Steffens, Lincoln 40
Stetson 26
Streets Dept 21
Studio 24 8
Suraya 15
Taller Puertorriqueño 20
Tastykakes 26
Tate, Omar 20
Tattooed Mom 18
Temple University 8, 45, 113
Tharpe, Sister Rosetta 32
Thee Phantom & the Illharmonic Orchestra 21
Thomas, Assata 9
Three Times Dope 7
Tildie's Toy Box 17
Tommy DiNic's 15
Uncle Bobbie's

Coffee and Books 8, 109
Underground Railroad 107
Urban Axes 19
Urban Jungle 17
Valley Forge 19
Van Pelt-Dietrich Library Center 66
Vedge 15
Venna Venturi House 31
Vernick Food & Drink 10
Vetri Cucina 7, 14, 54
Vile, Kurt 7
Vox Populi 19
Wanamaker Organ 9
War on Drugs 7
Warehouse on Watts 19
Warmdaddy's 14
Watson, Bryant "Sad Eye" 67
Weckerly's 10
Wei, Wesley 21
Weilbacher, Mike 21
Wellness 8, 17
West Philly Scrub 90
WHYY 6, 35
Wideman, John Edgar 6
Wissahickon Valley Park 55
Wm. Mulherin's Sons 8
Wynne, Walt 21
Yowie 16
Zagar, Isaiah 61
Zahav 14, 82

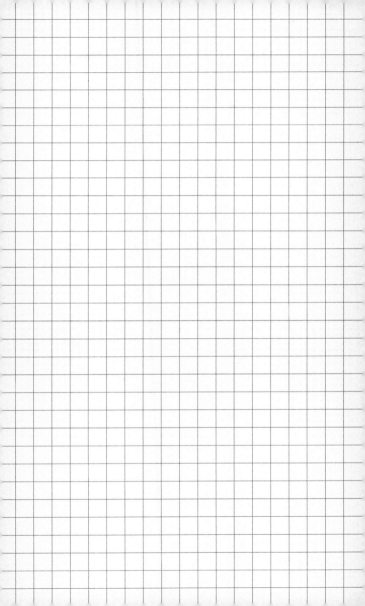

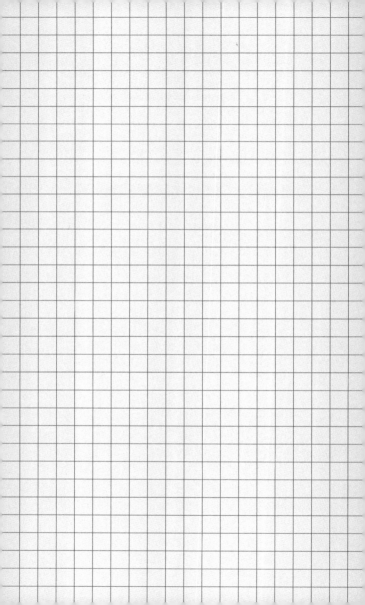

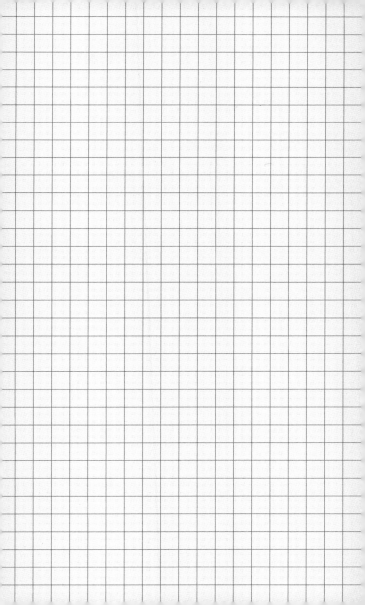

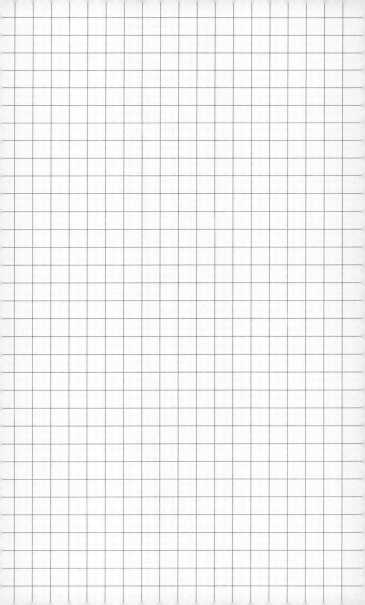

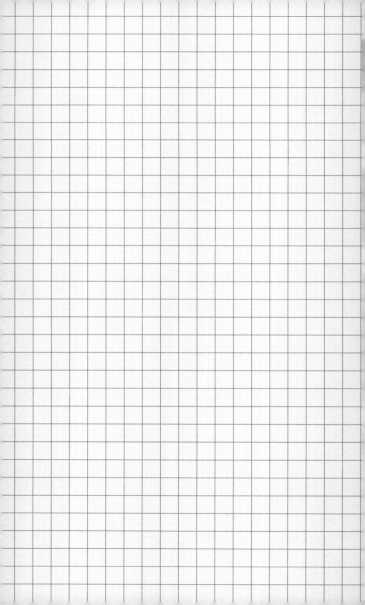

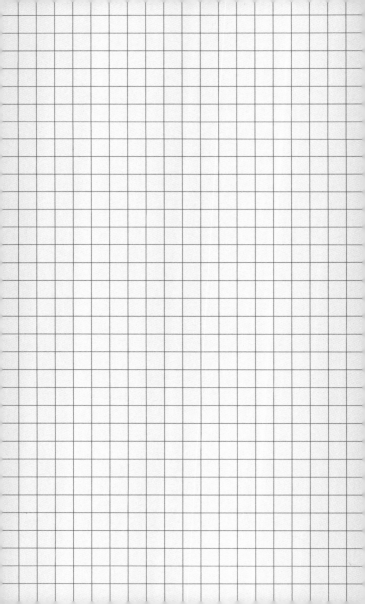

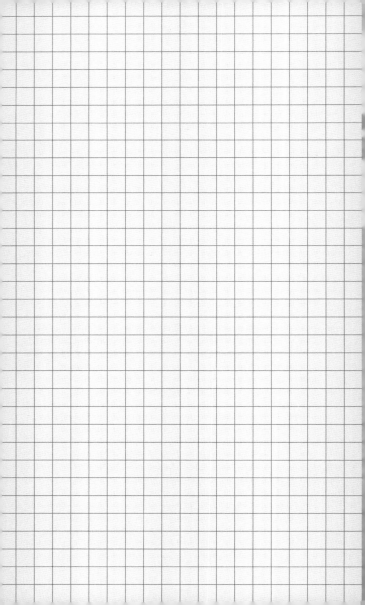

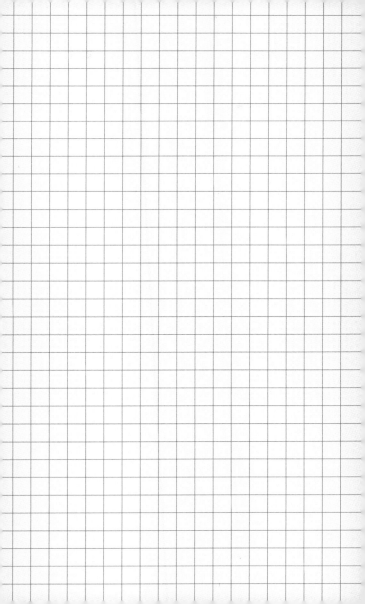

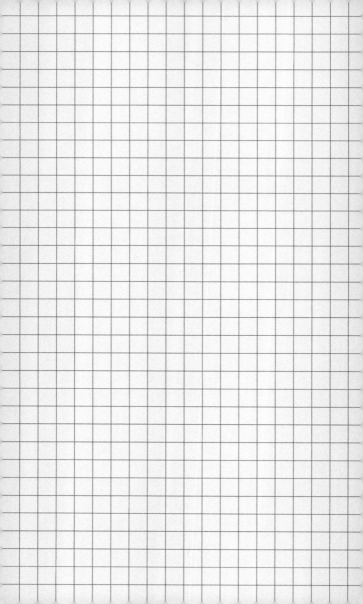

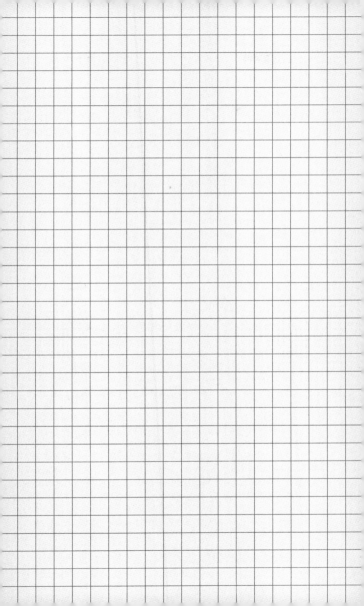

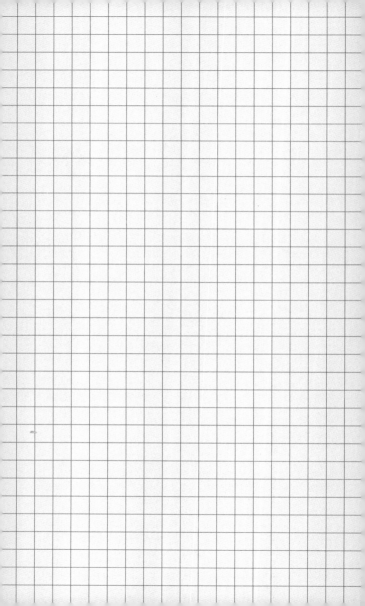

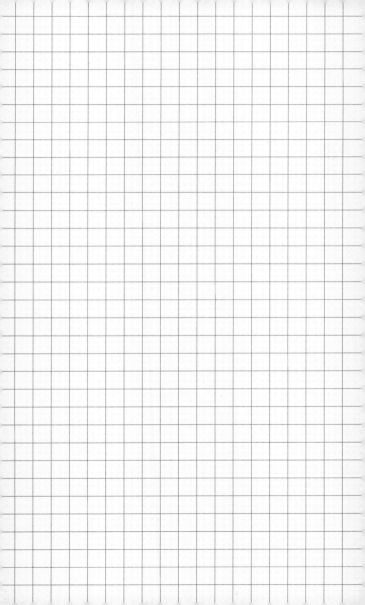

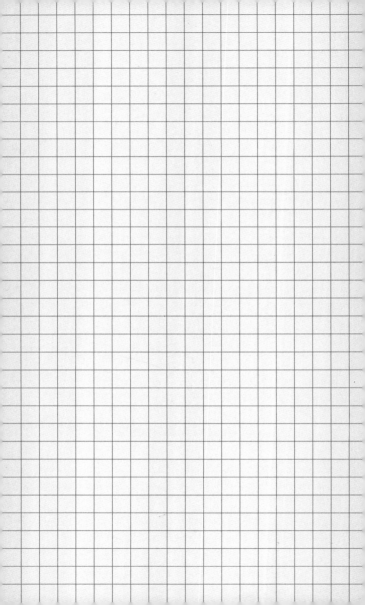